The Normal
SUPERNATURAL
Christian life

Aliss Cresswell

Published by FiftyFive Eleven Ltd

All Scripture quotations are taken from the
New International Version © 1973, 1978, 1984
by International Bible Society unless otherwise stated.

ISBN 13: 978-0-9572642-0-5
ISBN 10: 0-9572642-0-8

Published by FiftyFive Eleven Ltd

Printed in the USA

This book is available from
www.SpiritLifestyle.com
or email info@SpiritLifestyle.com

About the Author

Aliss Cresswell is an international speaker, business woman and 'miracle worker', training and equipping followers of Jesus to move in the supernatural realms and to impact the world with the love and power of the gospel. Aliss and her husband Rob are based in Chester, UK. They head up MorningStar Europe and have two children.

For more details visit
www.SpiritLifestyle.com
www.FaceBook.com/AlissCresswell

Contents

Introduction

Ten Liverpool ladies were on a day trip to Chester. As they alighted from the bus they noticed a blackboard propped up on a chair outside a shop which read, "FREE TODAY! HEALINGS & MIRACLES." Giggling, they nudged each other murmuring, "How bizarre to see such a sign on the High street." As they exchanged questioning glances, a woman popped her head out of the shop door and asked them, "Would any of you like a miracle?" They thought about it for a moment and one exclaimed, "Well I'm not feeling too good and would love to come in and sit down for a while."

Each of the women found a comfortable leather seat at the back of the shop where they discovered fresh coffee was served. All around them were charming items of furniture and gifts for sale with bookshelves full of Christian books and music. The volunteer working in the shop approached the ten women who by now were all sitting down wondering what was about to happen.

She asked if they had heard about the miracles Jesus was doing. "What a strange question," they thought. They had heard of Jesus but had not seen

Him do any miracles. The woman explained that Jesus took all their sin and sickness on the cross when He died, that He rose again and now has victory over death, and how they can be healed and forgiven through Jesus. She went on to ask who would like to go first.

One of the women began to explain that she was completely blind in her left eye. Apparently she had suffered an aneurism and a blood vessel had burst behind her eye a few years ago but there was nothing the doctors could do. She would never see again in that eye. She couldn't even see light. The shop volunteer placed her hand over the lady's eye and said, "In the name of Jesus I command this eye to see." She asked the lady to cover her good eye and describe what she could see through her blind eye. The woman was shocked! She could see light. Then she could see the silhouettes of her friends. The volunteer prayed again.

This time the woman with the blind eye was amazed to see some colours, she could describe what her friends were wearing and realised she could see almost perfectly out of her blind eye! She felt a strange peace, a wonderful sense of exhilaration and joy all at the same time. She realised Jesus had touched her and she was healed. One by one the whole group was prayed for, with dramatic results. The next lady was completely deaf in her left ear. She said that sadly her husband had died suddenly two years previously and the shock of it had caused her ear to lose all hearing.

The volunteer explained that it was probably an evil spirit causing the deafness and she told it to leave in the name of Jesus. Instantly the woman could hear again. She felt something leave and in its place was an overwhelming sense of belonging and wholeness.

Each of the ten women was healed instantly; one could not walk properly as the strength had left her legs and they kept giving way. The strength returned and she was able to put her stick away and walk and jump. Another had swollen ankles. As she watched, the swelling reduced before her very eyes. Another had suffered from sciatica for a long time. The pain left and she was able to bend with no more problems. The volunteer then asked the ladies from Liverpool if they knew Jesus. They all said "yes" and told her they were Roman Catholic, but they felt they knew Jesus so much better now since they had all received a touch from Him. They went on their way happy and healed, having encountered the Living God.

This is just one of many miracles taking place in our 'Spirit' shop in Chester and also our café in Blacon. This type of encounter can and should be an everyday part of a Christian's experience. The supernatural life as outlined in Mark 16 and Matthew 10 by Jesus and also demonstrated in Acts by the early church, should not be unusual but the norm for every follower of Jesus. When was the last time you led someone to Jesus? When did you last see a limb grow, cast out a demon or raise someone from the dead? How about, like Peter, leading 3,000 people to Jesus in one day?

This book has been written for every Christian who wants to see more of God's power at work in his or her life. I have included personal stories, funny incidents and teaching points, to help the reader find out not only what the Bible says on such topics as healing, casting out demons and spiritual authority, but also to learn how to put these into practice in everyday life and begin to walk in the supernatural on a daily basis.

The Apostle Paul wrote, "Now concerning the Spiritual, brothers, I do not want you to be ignorant or uninformed" (1 Corinthians 12:1). In most translations this verse reads, "Now concerning spiritual gifts brothers." However, in the original Greek text there is no word 'gifts'. The word translated 'spiritual' is 'pneumatikos' which also means *supernatural*. This verse could also be translated, "Now concerning the supernatural, brothers, I do not want you to be ignorant or uninformed." Many Christians are unfortunately ignorant about the supernatural. However many people who do not know Jesus are seeking to explore the supernatural by using 'illegal' ways to access the spiritual realm, that is, they are not entering through the door that is Jesus. We have prayed for unbelievers' eyes to be opened to the spiritual realm. As Christians who walk in the light, we need to lead them into the supernatural through Jesus. He is the Way, the Truth and the Life.

For years I asked the Lord to help me find someone who could teach me about the supernatural and mentor me, but there didn't seem to be anyone doing what I wanted to do. I soon discovered I had to rely on the Holy Spirit for help, make mistakes and try to learn from them as best I could. This book contains many of the lessons I have learned from the Holy Spirit and I hope that by sharing in some of my journey, you will avoid the pitfalls I made and that my ceiling will be a floor from which you can begin to walk out the normal supernatural Christian life.

Aliss Cresswell - April 2012

Chapter One

Flames of Fire

*"He makes winds his messengers,
flames of fire his servants"*

Flying back to England from Holland recently, I was sitting between two men. As the plane took off, I glanced out of the window to my left and noticed the guy next to me looked a bit uncomfortable. He appeared to be hot, his face was reddening and beads of sweat began to form on his forehead and run down his face. I thought perhaps he was afraid of flying and wondered if I should ask him if he wanted prayer. Before I had chance to say anything, he looked at me and said, "What *is* that?" I asked him what he meant. He said, "I feel so much power coming out of you and heat, it's like fire and it's burning me up. What is it?" I smiled and told him it was the power of God, the Spirit of Jesus that he could feel. He said he had tried many different religions and spiritual pathways but he had never before encountered anything like that. Before I had even spoken, he felt the fire of God emanating from me to such an extent it was making him sweat.

As we began chatting, I felt a pain at the base of my spine, so I asked him if he had any trouble with his lower back. He told me that fourteen years ago he had been involved in a bar fight and that his back had been broken. During surgery, metal pins had been inserted into some of the vertebrae to hold them together. He said he had constant pain in his back ever since, plus a trapped sciatic nerve which caused pain to surge down his leg. He was taking liquid morphine to try and help with the pain but it was constantly there. I asked him if he would like to experience some of the power of Jesus in his back and be healed. He said he would. I touched his shoulder with my finger and released the power of Jesus through the Holy Spirit and commanded the bones to reconstruct, the metal pins to come out and the pain to leave. He looked surprised as he had to admit all the pain had left instantly and when we were leaving the plane he told me he could move easily and the pain had not come back. He said it was the first time he had been pain free in fourteen years!

A few days later I was on another plane, this time with my husband in America. The flight attendant took her seat for landing which was adjacent to where I was sitting. Immediately she began to get hot and reached over for a newspaper to use as a fan. She kept blowing and fanning herself and wiping the sweat from her face. Rob and I exchanged knowing glances and smiled but didn't say a word.

"He makes winds his messengers, flames of fire his servants" (Psalm 104:4).

9 - 3 - 17 (Sun.)

My name, 'Alison' means 'sacred flame'. When I was a baby, the Minister at my parents' church dedicated me to the Lord and quoted Psalm 104:4. He prayed that I would be like a flame of fire and a messenger from God. I didn't know this until recently, but for many years I have felt a fire burning within me, and from an early age have introduced people to Jesus.

In the Presence of Angels

As I'm writing this I am aware of the presence of angels in the room. I have noticed that each time I welcome angels to work alongside me and thank God for them, for their protection over me and my family, for their care of me, I begin to be aware of other beings in the room with me, or walking alongside me. In a recent Sunday meeting we were talking about angels and people were sharing some of their experiences. As I began to share about an angel I had seen, a white feather floated down and landed in my Bible. This has happened on a number of occasions and other times I may feel the wind of their wings or hear unusual sounds in the room.

I was sitting in bed one morning a couple of years ago, chatting to the Lord as I normally do. I was aware of an angel that walked into the room through the outside wall of the house where there is a window overlooking the garden. I did not see him with my natural eyes but I knew he had come in. He walked to the foot of the four

15

poster bed and stood facing me with his hands out as though he had something for me.

So I placed my hands in front of me, palms upward in order to receive what he had to give. I thanked God for sending His messenger and I wanted whatever he had for me. In the spirit realm the angel placed a huge rusty key into my hands. I sensed that the key had not been used for a long time but knew that when I began to use it, the rust would disappear. A large shiny double-edged sword was also placed into my hands. At the time I didn't know what they represented but I asked the Holy Spirit to reveal to me what they were and what I was to do with them.

Soon afterwards the Lord told me that the key represented spiritual authority that He was giving me, also it was to unlock heavenly mysteries and that I was to help others understand how to use it. The sword was connected with Gideon (Judges 7:20), and I thought perhaps the angel could be the one that appeared to Gideon when he was threshing wheat in the winepress (see Judges 6).

Gideon and the Flames of Fire

In the account of Gideon, the Israelites were being oppressed by the Midianites. Midian means strife. The enemy was stealing from the people of God and forcing them to hide in caves. Gideon was scared and he was threshing wheat in a winepress, underground in a hidden place, where wheat threshing was difficult. The Israelites' crops were ruined and they were not fruitful or prosperous because they were living in fear of their enemy.

But the angel of the Lord appeared to Gideon and said, "The Lord is with you mighty warrior" (Judges 6:12). The angel that appeared to me in my bedroom was bringing the same message to the people of God. The Lord is with us and we are to arise as mighty warriors. Gideon felt insignificant and weak, but one of the reasons he became a mighty warrior and Judge of Israel, was that he believed what was spoken to him by the angel and obeyed the instructions given to him by the Lord. Obedience to the Holy Spirit is crucial. Gideon was fearful and did not believe he could do what was required of him. But God was with him and by obeying the Holy Spirit, no matter how ridiculous it seemed, he stepped out in faith and acted, knowing that if God did not perform a miracle, he and his tiny army would die.

We live in significant times and God is speaking to each one of us, declaring, "The Lord is with you mighty warrior." It is time to come out of hiding, out of those hidden, secret places. The Lord is lifting us up and placing us in full view of our enemy so that we can confront him. It is imperative that we follow the Lord's command to the letter, or we will not overcome. The enemy of the Lord has already been defeated; Jesus made a public spectacle of him. But we must know what is going on in heaven and obey the

Lord's instructions in order to see 'His Kingdom come on earth as it is in heaven.'

The Lord revealed the enemy's fear to Gideon by allowing him to overhear an account of a dream that the enemy had. We need to ask the Lord for revelation, to know the enemy's plans and for strategy and right timing from God. This is crucial. It is interesting to note that Gideon instructed his men to smash the jars they were holding and let their torches shine. Their weapons were no more than flames of fire and trumpets which they blew. It is time to let the fire shine out of us. Like a beacon on a hill, followers of Jesus are to be raised up in this hour for all to see.

At Gideon's word, the flaming torches were revealed, the trumpets were blown and the Midianites were thrown into confusion and killed one another! When we understand what is happening in the heavenly realms, follow God's instructions and reveal our true identity as sons of God (Galatians 3.26), it sends the enemy into confusion. We must blow our trumpets!

The Time is Now

As we begin to understand that we are indeed mighty warriors, and learn to walk in the authority that is available to us through Jesus, to let our light shine and bring the Kingdom of heaven to earth by demonstrating the power and love of God, increasingly we will find people falling to their knees and crying out, "What must I do to be saved?" We will witness instant healings and demons manifesting as we walk down the street, in our places of work and in our communities.

At the first ever meeting Rob and I held when we began our public ministry, the Lord spoke to me through two Scriptures in the book of Revelation and I prophesied from those verses. Recently the Lord spoke to me again about these verses and He told me to release it for this time.

"Then I saw a Lamb, looking as if it had been slain, standing in the centre of the throne, encircled by the four living creatures and the elders. He had seven horns and seven eyes, which are the seven spirits of God sent out into all the earth. He came and took the scroll from the right hand of him who sat on the throne. And when he had taken it, the four living creatures and the twenty-four elders fell down before the Lamb. Each one had a harp and they were holding golden bowls full of incense, which are the prayers of the saints" (Revelation 5:6-8).

"Another angel, who had a golden censer, came and stood at the altar. He was given much incense to offer, with the prayers of all the saints, on the golden altar before the throne. The smoke of the incense, together with the prayers of the saints, went up before God from the angel's hand. Then the angel took the censer, filled it with fire from the altar, and hurled it on the earth; and there came peals of thunder, rumblings, flashes of lightning and an earthquake" (Revelation 8:3-5).

A censer is a vessel for burning incense. God showed me that prayers of the saints have been filling the golden bowls like incense and as the bowls are filled, the angels throw them back down to earth with fire from the altar. It is time for us to receive answers to prayers that we have prayed for many years, and prayers that the church has prayed for centuries. We are also in a time where prayers will be answered quickly. Imagine a scenario and then see it unfold in front of your eyes. "The reaper will be overtaken by the plowman" (Amos 9:13).

As we continue through Revelation chapter 8, we see simultaneous judgments and answers to prayer. Fire speaks of burning up, unquenchable fire, calamities and earthquakes. The time we are in is not an easy time, but a time for overcoming from a place of rest. The promises in Revelation are for the overcomers.

Taking Back our Inheritance

Speaking at a meeting recently in South Florida, I asked a question, "Is there someone here whose shampoo and conditioner have gone missing out of the bathroom on more than one occasion?" The congregation must have thought I was crazy, that is until a woman and her two teenage daughters responded to the strange question. They walked to the front of the meeting and explained to everyone that they had bought shampoo and conditioner and placed it in their bathroom. The next day it had gone missing. In fact, this had happened two or three times recently and they couldn't work out what was happening. I thought perhaps that the enemy was trying to steal from them and asked them if he had stolen anything else from their lives, such as finances, relationships, health etc. Tears formed in their eyes as they confirmed that was exactly what had been happening. We prayed with them and broke off any curses and plans of the enemy to destroy their lives and declared that these things would be restored to them many times over.

We can pray and declare things in the spiritual realm and they will happen in the physical realm. They will happen quickly. God will answer our prayers in ways we could not even imagine. As we grow in spiritual authority we can declare that something will happen by a certain date. A woman who did not know anything about Jesus came into our 'Spirit' shop in Chester after seeing the sign outside for 'Free Miracles and Healing'. She told me her life was a mess and she had a house in France that had to be sold but she could not find a buyer. She was so desperate she had come in for a free miracle. I told her that was an easy thing for God to do. I prayed and declared that the house would be sold 'within two months'.

Less than two months later the same lady came back into our shop and left me a note. It said, "Dear Aliss, we passed your shop a couple of months ago and saw a sign outside saying 'Miracles Free Today'. You came to the door and asked us what miracle we needed. I asked for the house in France to sell. You prayed for it to sell within two months!! Well, it did!! I have an offer and by the end of this month it will be completely sold. Thank you very very much! You asked me to call back and let you know my miracle request had been granted, so today we came to see you to tell you. My life has been a living nightmare for the past six years and now thanks to you, Jesus and the Angels it's looking rosy. God bless you."

As we choose to lay our lives down and recognise with Paul that "I have been crucified with Christ and I no longer live" (Galatians 2:20), consumed by Holy Fire, the Spirit of Jesus, we can let that fire impact everything we touch and everyone we come into contact with, extending the Kingdom of Heaven as we go.

"For the message of the cross is foolishness to those who are perishing, but to us who are being saved it is the power (dynamite power, moral power, excellence of soul, power for performing miracles, power resting upon armies, strength, ability) of God" (1 Corinthians 1:18).

Peter's Revelation

The Apostle Peter moved in extraordinary miracles, signs and wonders, and after he received the baptism of the Holy Spirit he led at least 3,000 people to Jesus in one morning. Let us look at the circumstances leading up to those incredible years of his life.

Peter was a common man, he was a fisherman, uncouth and uneducated. He followed Jesus and operated under His anointing. Despite the fact that Peter loved Jesus and was full of faith, he was strong-willed and often operated in his own strength. Before Peter could be fully baptised in the Holy Spirit and power at Pentecost, his sinful nature needed to die. He had to experience the fire.

In Matthew 26:35 Peter declared to Jesus, "Even if I have to die with you, I will never disown you." We may love Jesus so much that we believe we would die for him, but Peter's loyalty to Jesus was tested. He actually denied Jesus three times on the night Jesus was arrested. Jesus looked straight at him and Peter "broke down and wept bitterly" (Luke 22:61,62). I wonder what happened when Peter looked into Jesus' eyes that night and what Peter saw in them. In Revelation 1:14, John describes Jesus' eyes as blazing fire.

When Jesus looked at Peter, I believe it was Holy Fire, the Holy Spirit that convicted him. When he really saw the state of his heart, Peter broke down in repentance and this experience humbled him from that moment on. The next time Peter saw Jesus was after the resurrection. Peter had changed. Jesus told him that he would die a martyr's death and Peter still chose to follow Him (see John 21:9).

"I have been crucified with Christ and I no longer live" (Galatians 2:20). We need to consider or reckon ourselves dead to sin (see Romans 6:11). The 'old' you is dead. Your old sinful nature has been crucified with Christ and you no longer live, but Christ lives in you and the life you now live, must be through faith in the Son of God (see Galatians 2:21). "Just as Christ was raised from the dead through the glory of the Father, we too may live a new life" (Romans 6:4). We need revelation of the fact that our old self is dead and we are now full of resurrection life and power.

Peter's understanding that his old self had died, needed to happen before he was able to receive the full baptism of the Holy Spirit and for revival to begin through him. The Lord wants this for His church. He is shaking all that can be shaken and bringing us to the end of ourselves. This is a time of repositioning and major shifting on this earth.

World Changers

If we truly want resurrection power and life, there first needs to be a death, or should I say a revelation of a death that has already happened (through Christ). In studying church history we see many revivals that were initiated by people who moved in supernatural power. It is interesting to note that as these revivalists understood their old self had been crucified with

Christ, and they were subsequently a new creation, they then began to demonstrate the Kingdom of God with signs and wonders. It was only then that they really understood what it was to be baptised with the Holy Spirit's fire and power.

Azusa Street Revival, Los Angeles 1906

Frank Bartleman wrote of this revival, "God has always sought a humble people. He can use no other... There is always much need for heart preparation, in humility and separation, before God can consistently come. The depth of any revival will be determined exactly by the spirit of repentance that is obtained. In fact, this is the key to every true revival born of God." (Quote taken from "Power to Change the World" by Rick Joyner).

This begins with a Spirit-initiated hunger for God before we even know Him, then a realisation of His holiness and our sinfulness. A recognition follows of what He has done for us at Calvary, that our sinful nature has been put to death. After this the Holy Spirit burns with passion within us for Jesus and we begin to cry out to be filled to the measure of all the fulness of God. God comes into our lives with the same power that spoke the universe into being, the same power that raised Jesus from the dead and He gives life to our mortal bodies (see Romans 8:11).

"For whoever wants to save his life will lose it, but whoever loses his life for me will find it" (Matthew 16:5).

The revivalist Smith Wigglesworth (1859-1947) said, "All His glory seems to fill the soul who is absolutely dead to self and alive to Him. There is so much talk about death, but I see that there is a death that is so deep in God that out of that death God brings the splendour of His life and all His glory."

If you are desperate for God to use you and move through you, hungry to see souls saved, wanting to do miracles, crying out to be walking in God's purpose for your life, then you need to know that you are a new creation. Your old self has been put to death and the resurrection power of Jesus lives in you. Why not let the past go and realise that Christ lives in you and the life you now live in the body you live by faith in the Son of God who loves you and gave Himself for you?" (see Galations 2:20). What if, instead of just asking God to send His Spirit and revive our nations or our communities, we also begin to use the power that is resident within us. Yield to the Holy Spirit, to the fire of God. You are a new creation and you have resurrection life. Use it.

It seems to me that the degree in which we operate in Holy Spirit power is directly related to the degree with which we know the reality of our old self being 'crucified with Christ'. The glorious power of the cross and Christ's resurrection is the very foundation of the power available to us. I believe it is also the foundation for the revival to which we are called to be a part.

If we can understand that our old self is gone, we can walk in the power of the Spirit, so full of His glory that demons will be cast out, sickness will not be able to remain and people will be so convicted by the Holy Spirit in us, they will fall to the ground and cry out for mercy. They will repent of their sin and will make Jesus Lord of their lives.

Smith Wigglesworth 'A True Prophet' March 1927

"The prophet's message is a word of the Lord that has become a burden upon the soul or a fire shut up in the bones, a burden, a pent-up fire, and anguish and a travail. The word of the Lord is a living flame – the symbol of Pentecost is a tongue of fire. Jeremiah had spoken his message, he felt that God had let him down and exposed him to ridicule and mockery. He would speak no more, but in the silence the fire burned in his bones. The fire consumed him until he could no longer hold, until one day the fire suddenly lept forth in forked lightning, or a flaming sword.

The moment comes when the prophet is full of power by the Spirit of the Lord. The fire constrains and consumes him and his generation persecute and despise his word. The Lord came to bring fire. He was straightened in Spirit but it was accomplished. So is every person who brings fire. There is a brooding, questioning, reasoning, excusing, hoping, fore-boding. The whole being is consumed. The very marrow burns. Speech may not or must not or will not come. Then in a moment suddenly it flames out. He becomes a voice through which another speaks. Fire compels attention; it announced itself and you don't have to advertise a fire. When the fire comes, the multitude come."

It is time for the prophets to arise. It is time for the preachers of the gospel to speak out. It is time for the flames of fire, the messengers of the Living God to go forth into this dark world and set it ablaze with the resurrection power and glory of Jesus Christ.

Chapter Two

Spiritual Authority

"I have given you authority...
to overcome all the power of the enemy"

I was travelling to Germany for a speaking engagement. It was a Saturday afternoon and I was to speak at a Healing Centre in Hanau for five nights, plus an international church on the Sunday morning and other places too, including taking teams onto the streets. I knew that as soon as I landed at Frankfurt Airport I would be driven to Hanau just in time to speak, with no time to spare.

I boarded the plane at Manchester airport. The aircraft was full, passengers had found their seats and buckled their seatbelts. We were preparing to taxi along the runway when the Captain made an announcement over the intercom: "I am very sorry to tell you that all the radar systems in the northern half of Germany have just shut down. It sounds as though it will be at least three hours before we can take off, but we'll keep you on the plane so that we can leave as soon as the problem is solved. I'll give you updates from time to time."

Understandably I was concerned, not least because I needed to be in Hanau to speak in a few hours' time, but also because I realised I didn't have a contact number for the people who were picking me up at the airport. I tried to call my husband Rob, but my phone wouldn't work! After a couple of minutes of wondering what to do, a realisation dawned on me. I have authority through Jesus in the spiritual realm, and what occurs in the spiritual realm affects the natural.

I sensed something was trying to prevent me entering Germany. Speaking out loud I said, "I take authority over the radar systems in the northern half of Germany and I command them to come back on in the name of Jesus." The man sitting next to me gave me a strange look and shook his head. He was probably wondering why he always ended up sitting next to the weirdo!

However, within a minute or two, the Captain's voice came back over the intercom, "Well, I'm surprised but very pleased to tell you that the radar systems are now working again and we will be taking off in the next few minutes." I just looked at the guy to my left and gave him a wry smile. Mmmm, not so crazy after all! The authority we have in the spiritual realm is immense. We must learn how to access and move in this authority.

During that week in Germany, there were incredible manifestations of glory, numerous healings and many salvations. In fact, we had so many that two new churches were established. It is so important to gain an understanding of spiritual authority. Without this you will struggle to move in any real supernatural power.

Why Bad Things Happen in this World

In the beginning God created the galaxies, the Universe and our world. The Bible says He made everything good. He created men and women who would live forever and be His children. He loved them and gave them authority to rule over the world "And God blessed them, and God said to them, Be fruitful, and multiply, and replenish the earth, and subdue it: and have dominion over the fish of the sea, and over the fowl of the air, and over every living thing that moves upon the earth" (Genesis 1:28 KJV).

Authority and submission go hand in hand. We only have delegated authority in any realm of life to the degree that we submit to the source of that power over us. Therefore in the UK a policeman only has authority over people to the degree that he himself submits to his commanding officers, they in turn to the Queen and she in turn to God. Adam and Eve had authority over the earth because they were in absolute submission to God who had granted them that power.

There was no death, no sin, no disease, no war nor famine. God loved His children and wanted them to love Him too and have a special, perfect relationship with Him. He gave them free will so they could choose to love Him. Love is not truly love unless it is given freely, so God gave them a choice that would enable them to trust Him; He said they could eat the fruit of any tree in the Garden of Eden except one, the tree of the knowledge of good and evil.

Satan had been cast out of heaven to earth for trying to take God's throne ("How you have fallen from heaven, O Lucifer, son of the dawn! You have been cast down to the earth" Isaiah 14:12). When he saw God's beautiful creation and beloved creatures, Satan seized an opportunity to take revenge. In the form of a serpent, he persuaded the man and woman to trust his word instead of God's word. Adam and Eve disobeyed God by eating the fruit of the forbidden tree. This was a terrible mistake. Adam and Eve had submitted to Satan and therefore surrendered their God-given authority to him. They had now, in effect, handed the keys of authority on the earth to Satan. Since that time, sin, death and disease have reigned in our world because of man's disobedience to God. We are all born into a fallen world, under the power of Satan and deserving of the penalty of death. The Bible says that Satan comes to "steal, kill and destroy" (John 10:10); most of us have experienced this in our lives! But the verse goes on to say that Jesus came to give us life to the full.

God's Plan for your Life

Because He loves you so much, God sent His only Son, Jesus into the world to be born and live as a man.

He had no sin because He was born of God and He lived a sinless life, completely submitted to his heavenly Father, but He chose to die on a cross and take all the punishment for our sin and disease. Seven hundred and fifty years before Jesus came to earth and died on a cross, a prophet named Isaiah prophesied this about Him: "He took up our sicknesses, weaknesses and distresses and carried our sorrows and pains... He was pierced for our transgressions, He was crushed for our guilt and iniquities; the punishment that brought us peace was upon Him, and by His wounds we are healed and made whole" (Isaiah 53).

Before Jesus was crucified He said to His followers, "I will give you the keys of the Kingdom of Heaven" (Matthew 16:19). The Bible says that when Jesus died He went into hell and took back the keys of authority from Satan. "And having disarmed the powers and authorities, he made a public spectacle of them, triumphing over them by the cross" (Colossians 2:15). Jesus was raised from the dead, having defeated death, sin, sickness and all the powers of darkness. In Revelation 1:18 Jesus says "I am the Living One; I was dead, and look, I am alive forever and ever. And I hold the keys of death and hell." He conquered Satan and all the powers of darkness.

Jesus has the keys of authority over all. To every person who follows Him, He gives the keys of authority over the earth and over all the power of Satan. "I have given you authority to trample on snakes and scorpions and to overcome all the power of the enemy; nothing will harm you" (Luke 10:19).

Keys of the Kingdom

"And I will give you the keys of the kingdom of heaven, and whatever you bind on earth will be bound in heaven, and whatever you loose on earth will be loosed in heaven" (Matthew 16:18,19). The word used here for 'bind' in the original Greek means to bind, forbid or prohibit. We can forbid evil spirits from operating and prohibit Satan's plans from being accomplished in our lives and in the lives of those we meet. The word 'loose' in the Greek means to set free, release from chains, break up an assembly, to deprive of authority, to declare unlawful, break up, demolish, destroy, to overthrow and do away with. Wow! If we are submitted to the authority of Jesus, as His Church, He says He will give us the keys of authority to destroy the works of Satan, break up wicked assemblies, prohibit unlawful activities from taking place and set people free who have been held captive by the enemy. We need to wake up and recognise just what authority has been given to us and learn how to use it.

So in the beginning God gave us authority over the earth. We gave it away to Satan, but Jesus won it back and He gives authority over the earth to those who follow Him. As we submit our lives to Jesus, we can use the authority He has given us.

Recognising the Authority of Jesus

In Matthew 16:16-19 we read about a conversation Jesus had with one of His followers, Peter. Jesus asked Peter who people said He was. The answer that Peter gave, "You are the Christ, the Son of the Living God" was revealed to Peter by Father God. "Jesus replied, "Blessed are you, Simon son of Jonah, for this was not revealed to you by man, but by my Father in heaven. And I tell you that you are Peter, and on this rock I will build my church, and the gates of Hades will not overcome it." Jesus makes a word play on Peter's name, which means 'rock', but the rock or foundation upon which Jesus says He will build his church is not a man but a revelation of who Jesus is. The foundation of the church is the revelation from the Father that Jesus is the Christ, the Son of the Living God.

Hell (or Hades) has gates (see Matthew 16:18). There are keys to those gates (see Revelation 1:18). These gates represent the consequence and influence of sin and death on the earth. We need to lock and unlock hell's gates with those keys. This is a twofold work, firstly to see people saved through the gospel of Jesus Christ (released from punishment) and secondly to stem (or lock up) the influence of Satan's influence on the earth.

As we have just seen, one of the ways we use those keys is by receiving revelation from heaven and then bringing to earth what we know to be happening in heaven, preventing Satan's purposes on the earth from being fulfilled and setting captives free. One of the primary ways we do this is by speaking and acting out what we sense the Lord is saying and doing in heaven. Heaven has gates and doors too. "After this I looked, and there before me was a door standing open in heaven. And the voice I had first heard speaking to me like a trumpet said, 'Come up here'" (Revelation 4:1). We need to know that we are "seated in heavenly places" (see Ephesians 2:6) and learn to use our spiritual senses to understand what is happening in heaven and to bring the Kingdom of heaven onto the earth. Revelation and heavenly downloads are strategic keys and we need to know how to use them.

I will go on to explain in further chapters some of the ways in which we see what is going on in heaven and how to bring it onto this earth.

Keys in Germany

One time when I was speaking in Germany, near Bonn, I stayed in a hotel and the room I was given was number 22. Apparently the visiting preacher who stayed there before me had the same room. I asked the Lord what this meant.

He reminded me of Isaiah 22:22 so I looked it up. "I will place on his shoulder the key to the house of David; what he opens no one can shut, and what he shuts no one can open." I sensed the Lord saying to me, "Would you like a key to Germany?" I wasn't sure what that meant, but I replied that yes I would. I didn't think any more about it until a few months later when I was sitting on the aeroplane on my way to Hanau and the radar systems went down. After that incident I realised the Lord had given me authority in the spiritual realm, to impact such things in the natural realm as radar systems (which also speak of listening and communication devices). Of course, I realised that I didn't have the only key for Germany. Keys are available to each one of us as we follow Jesus, but we don't always know how to access and use them. We need to use the keys we have, not just collect them. There is much to learn and I'm only just beginning. What an exciting journey we are on!

Authority and Responsibility

I love this Scripture written by the Apostle Paul: "I pray also that the eyes of your heart may be enlightened in order that you may know the hope to which he has called you, the riches of his glorious inheritance in the saints, and his incomparably great power for us who believe. That power is like the working of his mighty strength, which he exerted in Christ when he raised him from the dead and seated him at his right hand in the heavenly realms, far above all rule and authority, power and dominion, and every title that can be given, not only in the present age but also in the one to come. And God placed all things under his feet and appointed him to be head over everything for the church, which is his body, the fullness of him who fills everything in every way" (Ephesians 1:18-23).

I have heard Rick Joyner say, "There can be no true authority without responsibility." I remember one time asking the Lord for spiritual authority over a place that He had put on my heart, the neighbourhood of Blacon, a suburb of Chester well known locally for its crime and drugs. At the time we were living in a pretty village a couple of miles away. The Lord told me, "To the degree you take responsibility for this neighbourhood is the degree to which I will give you spiritual authority over it." Not long after this, the Holy Spirit asked me to give up my career, so I did. It meant laying down a well paid job - a business venture I had established, and therefore also my dream home. Then He asked me to work in Blacon for no pay, reaching people with the love and power of the gospel of Jesus. So I did that and many were touched by Jesus and gave their lives to Him.

A while later we began a church in Blacon. Soon after this, the Holy Spirit asked us to live in Blacon, so we sold our house in the village and moved. It was around this time that a demonic principality in the form of a man appeared to me on our neighbour's roof. It was trying to frighten me from moving to the area and starting a church there, but I assumed it was much more scared of me, that was why it manifested! Demonic spirits often manifest in a last resort to intimidate when there is a critical battle for territorial possession about to take place (see Matthew 4).

Our family of four required a certain level of income, I wasn't being paid and Rob really needed to earn a full time wage. However, we sensed the Holy Spirit say that Rob should only work a paid job two days per week. This seemed impossible to us, but we knew that if we would be obedient to the Lord, He would look after us. So Rob agreed to work for a local charity two days each week and the rest of the time we asked the Holy Spirit what He wanted to do that particular day; we waited on Him for visions or a sense of where we should go and we would begin to talk to people and demonstrate the Kingdom of God with power.

One day we felt we should go to the local shops in Blacon. As it so happened we were outside the building that has since become home to our café. We had taken along a young student from a local school of evangelism who wanted to see what we did. I turned to Rob and asked if he had received anything from the Lord that morning. He said, "Not much, just 'pink tracksuit'." I said, "Oh, you don't see many of those these days do you!?"

We began to walk towards the shops and, standing directly in front of us were two women, one of whom was wearing a pink tracksuit. We approached the women and told them we were Christians and God wanted to do a miracle in their lives that day. They were surprised and one said, "That's incredible! I was just saying that she needs a miracle," pointing to the woman wearing the pink tracksuit.

Rob was able to show them his journal where he had written the words, 'pink tracksuit' and another word of knowledge to do with her stomach/hip area. She told us she was expecting her fifth child, the father was not her husband and her other children had been taken into care. She was a heroin addict in her early twenties. The other woman had recently come off heroin and crack cocaine but was struggling.

We told them about Jesus and they both began to confess their sin and ask Jesus to be Lord of their lives. The five of us held hands as the two women prayed, standing outside the row of shops. People began to stare at us, but the women were oblivious as they knelt on the pavement and asked us to keep praying, saying they wanted more of God. We prayed that the Holy Spirit would come and fill them.

How amazing! Not long after this event occurred, we heard that the girl in the pink tracksuit had died soon after giving birth. I thank God that Rob had waited on the Lord that morning and had been obedient to the Holy Spirit. I believe she is now with the Lord.

Levels of Authority

Just as there are levels of authority in this world, so also there are levels of authority in the spiritual realm. As we obey the Holy Spirit, take responsibility and learn to live by Kingdom principles, we will grow in spiritual authority.

Soon after starting up the church in Blacon, we opened a tiny café. The same week we opened the café, I began to realise just what authority we have been given through Jesus. I had been praying for revival for so many years, but I decided that week that I would just go ahead and start revival everywhere I went. The amazing miracles of healings, salvations and people being set free from demons broke out at the same time and haven't stopped. In fact, now it is not only me doing the miracles, but they're breaking out all over the place. Do you realise that when you are contending for something in your life, when you finally see it breaking out, it is not just for your benefit? Many others will be able to step into the realms that you have opened up, whether that be in something like healings, signs and wonders, salvations, music, creativity, justice, business, education or science.

One of the many things I have learned is, DO NOT GIVE UP! If there is a price to breakthrough it is the cost of perseverance. The rewards are great!

The Bible says:

For Christ died for sins once for all, the righteous for the unrighteous, to bring you to God. Jesus humbled himself and became obedient to death - even death on a cross. Therefore God exalted him to the highest place and gave him the name that is above every name, that at the name of Jesus every knee should bow, in heaven and on earth and under the earth. Having disarmed the powers and authorities, he made a public spectacle of them, triumphing over them by the cross. He says, I am the Living One; I was dead, and behold I am alive for ever and ever! And I hold the keys of death and hell.

You are saved by the resurrection of Jesus Christ, who has gone into heaven and is at God's right hand - with angels, authorities and powers in submission to Him. For in Christ all the fullness of the Deity lives in bodily form, and you have been given fullness in Christ, who is the Head over every power and authority. Jesus says, All authority in heaven and on earth has been given to me. Therefore, go into all the world and preach the good news to all creation. And these signs will accompany you who believe: In my name you will drive out demons, you will place your hands on sick people and they will get well.*

*1 Peter 3:18, Philippians 2:8-10, Colossians 2:15, Revelation 1:18, 1 Peter 3:21-22, Colossians 2:9-10, Matthew 28:18, Mark 16:15-18

Chapter Three

The Holy Spirit

*"In order to begin a revival through us
the Lord must start a revival in us"*

In 1995 I gave birth to a stillborn daughter at nine months of pregnancy. As you can imagine it was an awful experience to go through, but I chose to throw myself on God and to follow Jesus with all my heart. I felt the presence of God like no other time before and surprised non-believers by the peace and joy I experienced despite the loss of our daughter, knowing that we would see her again one day.

Just a few years ago, I was shopping at Asda supermarket. For no apparent reason I began to think about my daughter who had died years earlier and tears filled my eyes. Obviously it was sad and I often think of her now, but to think of her at the supermarket seemed out of place sixteen years on.

I wondered if there was another reason for me feeling the way I did. Perhaps I was near someone who'd had a similar experience, but the only person close by was a woman on the checkout and she looked too old to have recently given birth. But the feeling wouldn't go away and the more I thought about the woman on the checkout, the more emotional I felt. I decided it could be the Lord, although I wasn't sure and knew I would be taking a risk, especially on a subject so emotive. But I remembered hearing a phrase that John Wimber would say, "Faith is spelt R-I-S-K," and I thought the worst that could happen is I could be wrong and look stupid (and that would be good for my pride), so I decided to go for it.

I began to tremble as I tried to choose my words carefully and approached the woman with, "Hi, a number of years ago I had a baby who was stillborn and I just began thinking about her. I'm a Christian and wondered if God was showing me that someone else has gone through a similar experience. I could be wrong, but I don't suppose you have lost a grandchild recently have you?"

She looked at me in disbelief. She said, "Do I look sad?" to which I replied that she didn't. But then she went on to tell me that her son's partner had given birth to a baby the previous day and the baby died. I was astounded and began to weep as I inwardly thanked God for His mercy towards me and felt compassion for the woman in front of me. She began to cry too. I couldn't help but tell her about God's love for her and her family, how Satan brings death but Jesus died for her and rose again and wants to give her life. With a line of people now formed behind me, but oblivious to their stares, I took the woman's hands in mine and together we prayed for the Prince of Peace to be made known in her household. She asked God to forgive her sins and invited Jesus into her life.

She then told me how her husband was seriously ill with leukaemia and it was his birthday that day. I prayed for healing for him, gave her some booklets and headed for home. A couple of weeks later I saw her again and this time she was radiant, telling me how her family were recovering well and her husband had been to see the consultant who was surprised to report that the leukaemia had not only stabilised but was regressing! We thanked God for His goodness.

Learning How to Pay Attention

As I reflected on that experience, I realised I could so easily have missed hearing the voice of the Holy Spirit. In the supermarket that day, He was showing me someone that He wanted to touch with the Kingdom of Heaven, to bring hope and healing. Because He spoke to me through an emotion and my own feelings, I could have begun to feel sad that my daughter had died and got under some sort of depression when really it was the Holy Spirit speaking to me about someone else.

We need to develop a close relationship with the Holy Spirit and understand some of the ways in which He communicates with us. I have told Him I'm sorry for the many times I must have misheard Him or assumed He had nothing to say.

In other chapters I will expand on various ways in which the Lord speaks to us, but for now I want to encourage you to fall in love with the Holy Spirit. He is God. He is love. It is good to honour the Holy Spirit, to worship Him and invite Him to spend each day and night with you. Speaking of the Holy Spirit, Jesus said, "And I will ask the Father and he will give you another Counsellor to be with you forever - the Spirit of truth. The world cannot accept him because it neither sees him nor knows him. But you know him for he lives with you and will be in you" (John 14:16,17).

The night before He was crucified, Jesus said "But I tell you the truth; it is for your good that I am going away. Unless I go away, the Counsellor will not come to you; but if I go, I will send him to you" (John 16:7).

Jesus was to go back to Heaven to be at the right hand of the Father, then He could send the Counsellor, His Holy Spirit to us, to live with us, in us and to anoint us. It is better that we have the Holy Spirit here with each of us in person than to have Jesus before He was glorified.

I love to read about past revivalists and hear their stories and I noticed a common thread amongst a number of them. Those who were moving in unusual power, seeing many miracles, planting churches, leading thousands to Christ and raising the dead all had a close relationship with the Holy Spirit. They would talk to Him as a friend, they obeyed Him even if it seemed strange to them and despite others trying to dissuade them.

I also noticed whilst reading the book of Acts that the Apostles would say, "It seemed good to the Holy Spirit and to us" or "...having been kept by the Holy Spirit from..." which seems to suggest that the Holy Spirit was always being consulted and spoke to them as a friend would. We need to get to know the Holy Spirit more than we already do. I love the Holy Spirit, He is my best friend, He is the Spirit of Jesus. I love His presence and power, the way He makes me feel, the words He whispers to me and the incredible things He shows me.

Discover what some of the greatest revivalists in history have said about their own experiences of the Holy Spirit:

Charles Finney (1792-1875)

Charles Finney is credited with leading over half a million people to Jesus. The Holy Spirit worked powerfully through him in the United States and Western Europe. One of the major revivalists of the nineteenth Century, Finney had a career as a lawyer, when one morning in a forest he 'gave his heart to God.' Later that day, back at the law office, he received a wonderful baptism of the Holy Spirit. He describes the experience in his own words, "...My heart seemed to be liquid within me... There was no fire, and no light in the room; nevertheless it appeared to me as if it were perfectly light. As I went in and shut the door after me, it seemed as if I met the Lord Jesus Christ face to face... I returned to the front office, and found that the fire that I had made of large wood was nearly burned out. But as I turned and was about to take a seat by the fire, I received a mighty baptism of the Holy Ghost. Without any expectation of it, without ever having the thought in my mind that there was any such thing for me, without any recollection that I had ever heard the thing mentioned by any person in the world, the Holy Spirit descended upon me in a manner that seemed to go through me, body and soul. I could feel the impression, like a wave of electricity, going through and through me. Indeed it seemed to come in waves and waves of liquid love; for I could not express it in any other way. It seemed like the very breath of God. I can recollect distinctly that it seemed to fan me, like immense wings.

No words can express the wonderful love that was shed abroad in my heart. I wept aloud with joy and love; and I do not know but I should say, I literally bellowed out the unutterable gushings of my heart. These waves came over me, and over me, and over me, one after the other, until I recollect I cried out, "I shall die if these waves continue to pass over me." I said, "Lord, I cannot bear any more"; yet I had no fear of death." (Quote taken from 'Memoirs' by Charles Finney).

The same day, an Elder of the church was brought in to check on Finney as he was behaving strangely. As soon as Finney began to describe what had happened, the Holy Spirit caused the elder to laugh for some time, despite the fact that he was usually a serious man!

Smith Wigglesworth (1859-1947)

Wigglesworth was a revivalist from Bradford, Yorkshire in England. He witnessed incredible miracles and raised many from the dead. He speaks here of a time early in his ministry when he was baptised with the Holy Spirit:

"I was as certain as possible that I had received the Holy Ghost and was absolutely rigid in this conviction... But as the days passed I became more and more hungry... Mrs Boddy (the Vicar's wife) laid her hands on me and the fire fell.... I knew I had received the Spirit's incoming that the apostles received at Pentecost. I knew that everything I had had up to that time was in the nature of an anointing bringing me in line with God in preparation, but now I knew I had the Biblical baptism in the Spirit."

After this experience, Wigglesworth went home and told his wife, but she believed that they became filled with the Holy Spirit when they gave their lives to Jesus and that they didn't need 'the baptism.' He tried to convince her otherwise. Up until that point, Smith had problems preaching, he was not good at speaking in public and just couldn't seem to get his words out. So his wife told him to preach that Sunday to prove to her that the baptism in the Holy Spirit would make a difference. To her astonishment, he spoke so well that she was heard to say, "That's not my Smith, that can't be my Smith" as he was speaking. One after another, as the power of God was made manifest in the meeting, people were knocked off their seats onto the floor. It was then that she was convinced there was more to be had than she had experienced up to that point.

After being baptised with the Holy Spirit, Smith Wigglesworth operated out of such power that people were convicted of their sin wherever he went, he did thousands of miracles of healing and saw many people raised from the dead. One of my favourite stories is the time he was travelling by train and he was sitting reading his Bible. Not long before the train journey came to an end, he got up to go to the bathroom. Those sitting near him fell to their knees and explained that something about him convicted them of their sin. It was the Holy Spirit, the Spirit of Jesus. So he told them about Jesus and they gave their lives to Him. That's what I want!

John G Lake (1870-1935)

For ten years before his baptism in the Holy Spirit, John G Lake operated in a level of healing far and above anything that most of us have seen. He was assured by many people that he had a beautful baptism in the Holy Spirit but he was not satisfied with the level of anointing that he had. It did not answer the cry of his heart.

The story of his baptism in the Holy Spirit is wonderful. One day Lake was asked to pray with a lady confined to a wheelchair who had inflamatory rheumatism for ten years. He took a friend of his with him. Lake had been asking the Lord to baptise him with the Holy Spirit for some time and had been fasting for ten months particularly asking for this. Whilst his friend was talking to the lady about healing, Lake sat in the corner of the room and described how "currents of power began to rush through my being from the crown of my head to the soles of my feet. The shocks of power increased in rapidity, and voltage. As these currents of power would pass through me, they seemed to come upon my head, rush through my body, and through my feet into the floor." His body was vibrating as his friend called him over to pray with the lady. As soon as he put his hand on the woman, the power of God flowed through Lake, through the woman who was instantly healed, and hit his friend with such force that he was thrown backwards. His friend announced, "John, I think you have been baptised with the Holy Spirit now."

Kathryn Kuhlman (1907-1976)

Healing evangelist Kathryn Kuhlman said "At the end of a dead-end street, four o'clock on Saturday afternoon – in that moment when I yielded to Him body, soul and spirit, when I gave Him everything, all there was of me, I knew then what the Scripture meant, 'If any man will follow me, let him take up his cross'. The cross is always the sign, the symbol, of death. That afternoon Kathryn Kuhlman died. Now I have experienced the baptism of the Holy Spirit... but there are still people today who speak with an unknown tongue who have never been baptised in the Holy Spirit! When you are completely filled with the Holy Spirit, baptised in the Holy Spirit, there will be a crucifying of the flesh.... you will die. And there are a lot of professing Christians, professing to being filled with the Holy Spirit, who have never died to the flesh. .. When I died, He came in; I was baptised, I was filled with His spirit, I spoke with an unknown tongue as He took every part of me... Then, for the first time, I realised what it meant to have power... We don't have to pray for miracles – there will automatically be miracles." (Quote taken from 'Daughter of Destiny' by Jamie Buckingham).

In order to begin a revival *through* us, the Lord wants to begin a revival *in* us.

The Apostle Peter

In the chapter 'Flames of Fire', we discussed the Apostle Peter and how he came to know the fire of God in his life. Soon after Peter's revelation, the baptism of the Holy Spirit and power came at Pentecost. Peter's ministry began. He preached in the power of the Holy Spirit, the people were cut to the heart and 3,000 were saved. He counted his old sinful nature as being dead, and was able to operate with such power of the Spirit that even his shadow healed the sick and cast out demons (see Acts 5:15).

Jesus Operated in the Power of the Holy Spirit

Jesus was a man when He lived on the earth and He did no miracles until after the Holy Spirit came upon Him at His baptism (see Matthew 3:16 and John 2:11). Full of the Holy Spirit, He was able to overcome Satan when He was tempted in the wilderness. The Bible says of Jesus, "For he is sent by God. He speaks God's words, for God's Spirit is upon him without measure or limit" (John 3:34 NLT).

Jesus said to His followers, "As the Father has sent me, I am sending you. And with that he breathed on them and said, 'Receive the Holy Spirit'" (John 20:21). We are like the man Jesus in this world. We can do nothing without the power of the Holy Spirit. But we have the potential of the fullness of the Holy Spirit living within us. "And if the Spirit of him who raised Jesus from the dead is living in you, he who raised Christ from the dead will also give life to your mortal bodies through his Spirit, who lives in you" (Romans 8:11). We have the same Holy Spirit in us that raised Jesus Christ from the dead.

In John 14:12, as Jesus talked about the miracles He was doing, He said, "I tell you the truth, anyone who has faith in me will do what I have been doing. He will do even greater things than these, because I am going to the Father." The disciples performed miracles under the anointing of Jesus but just before Jesus ascended to heaven after His death and resurrection, He told them to remain in Jerusalem until they had been clothed with power from on high; that is the power of the Holy Spirit.

"But when he, the Spirit of truth, comes, he will guide you into all truth. He will not speak on his own; he will speak only what he hears, and he will tell you what is yet to come. He will bring glory to me by taking from what is mine and making it known to you. All that belongs to the Father is mine. That is why I said the Spirit will take from what is mine and make it known to you" (John 16:13-15).

I want to be like Jesus. In Acts 10:38 we read "how God anointed Jesus of Nazareth with the Holy Spirit and power, and how he went around doing good and healing all who were under the power of the devil, because God was with him." Sometimes I quote that verse to myself and replace Jesus' name with my name and city. If I ever have a tombstone, I'd like that to be on it!

Honour the Holy Spirit

The Lord is particularly protective of the Holy Spirit. On different occasions we read not to "resist the Holy Spirit" (Acts 7:51), "Do not quench the Holy Spirit", "Do not grieve the Holy Spirit" (Ephesians 4:30) and not to speak against the Holy Spirit (Matthew 12:32). When Ananias and Sapphira lied to the Holy Spirit it had fatal consequences for them (see Acts 5). The Holy Spirit is sensitive. We must be sensitive to Him. He wants us to know how He is feeling and He wants to share with us what is happening in heaven and He will take us there, He will open up the spiritual realm to us and show us things we have not experienced before. He knows all things and speaks only what He hears in heaven. I love the Holy Spirit.

The Holy Spirit has many forms, such as the Spirit of Wisdom (who is referred to in Scripture in the feminine), the Spirit of Might, the Spirit of Revelation (see Proverbs 3, Isaiah 11:2, Ephesians 1:17).

In the second chapter of Acts we read how the Holy Spirit came at Pentecost and baptised all the believers who were waiting for Him to come. This happened ten days after Jesus had gone back to be with the Father in heaven. Jesus knew that He had only been able to do what He did on earth because He was full of the Holy Spirit, and likewise He knew that His followers needed to be filled with the Holy Spirit in order to accomplish all that He had called them to do. The same applies to us. In fact, one of the main reasons Jesus went to the cross was so we could be the dwelling place of God, that we could carry the presence of God, the Holy Spirit within us. Isn't that incredible?

Getting to know the Holy Spirit

I love the Holy Spirit. I talk to Him all the time. The more you fall in love with Him and talk to Him, the more you will understand His ways and how He communicates with us. "He will guide you into all truth." Pay attention to what He says to you. It would be simpler if the Holy Spirit spoke with a loud audible voice but that is rare. Usually He speaks quietly, when we're close to Him. It may be that you feel compassion for someone you see. That is usually the Holy Spirit's compassion you are feeling, and He is prompting you to pray for them or go and speak to them.

The Holy Spirit will show you what to say. "Just say whatever is given you at the time, for it is not you speaking, but the Holy Spirit" (Mark 13:11). This verse is in the context of those who are arrested and brought to trial, but it applies any time you are speaking and needing help to know what to say. In fact, if we are to live the normal supernatural Christian life, it applies any time we open our mouths!!

John the Baptist was filled with the Holy Spirit from birth (see Luke 1:15) and I believe that our children can be filled with the Holy Spirit too. Pray for your children whilst still in the womb and as they are growing. Lay your hands on them and ask the Holy Spirit to come and fill them and bring them into a relationship with Jesus.

We read in Acts 2 that when Jesus' followers were baptised with the Holy Spirit, they began to speak in other languages or tongues. Just the other day this happened with a twenty year old girl in our shop, and as she was praying and giving her life to Jesus she began to speak out words that were not English. I asked her if she knew what she was saying but she said she had no idea but it felt good, that something was coming up from within her and she had to let the words out. I explained that it was a heavenly language from the Holy Spirit. (Sometimes it is an actual language, like Chinese, that a person from that particular country would understand, and other times it is a heavenly language). Bits of gold dust, like glitter began to appear over her neck and she felt what she described as a 'draught of happiness'.

This sort of thing should be normal in our everyday lives. If you have the same Holy Spirit living in you that raised Jesus from the dead and created the heavens and the earth, then you can release the Kingdom of Heaven wherever you go. You can raise the dead. You can heal the sick. You can preach the good news of the Kingdom of God. You can cleanse the lepers. You can cast out demons. Start practising. See what happens. Never give up. The whole of heaven is behind you and within you, cheering you on.

The Nature of the Holy Spirit

The Holy Spirit is God. In the beginning He hovered over the deep and created the Universe. In the Old Testament He came upon people for specific tasks, such as delivering Israel from her enemies, but it was prophesied many times that the Holy Spirit would be given to all, in greater measure. That was always God's plan. "I will pour out my Spirit on all people; your sons and daughters will prophesy, your old men will dream dreams, your young men will see visions. Even on my servants, both men and women, I will pour out my Spirit in those days" (Joel 2:28). "For I will pour water on the thirsty land and streams on dry ground; I will pour out my Spirit on your offspring, and my blessing on your descendants..." (Isaiah 44:3). "And I will put my Spirit in you and move you to follow my decrees..." (Ezekiel 36:27). God's purpose was always for us to be filled with His Holy Spirit, to be the Temple of His Holy Spirit, to carry His glory, His presence.

The Holy Spirit Reveals Jesus

I am sitting in my office above our 'Spirit' shop in Chester as I write this. I was supposed to be shut away so I could finish this book, but I went downstairs as there were some teenagers asking for me. They are friends of the teenager who had broken his knuckle a couple of years ago and came into the shop and watched his knuckle reconstruct as we prayed for it. He and his friends then gave their lives to Jesus and prayed for another guy to be healed. A couple of these teenagers came into the shop today and said, "Can you do that thing with us where we all hold hands and ask Jesus to come into our lives?"

There were eight or ten of them. I explained how Jesus loves them and died for them and rose from the dead, and how He has victory over sin, death and disease. We all stood and held hands as they asked God to forgive them and to come into their lives. We captured the moment on video. Then they asked the Holy Spirit to come and described a wonderful feeling. One said he couldn't stand and was hardly able to walk out of the shop later, another felt fire in his feet, one felt something in his chest, another said his body was tingling and a girl said it was as though the floor was vibrating under her feet. Some were giggling and others were crying, the presence of the Holy Spirit felt strong.

These are just some of the many ways we can experience the Holy Spirit. When I pray with someone I usually ask them what they are feeling. Perhaps if their feet feel on fire it could be that they are going to be someone who tells others about Jesus: "how beautiful are the feet of those on the mountain who bring good news" (Isaiah 52:7). I may then begin to declare that purpose over them and pray for boldness and for an anointing for that person to lead many to Jesus.

Sometimes the person I'm praying for may begin to feel dizzy or perhaps they have a headache that has suddenly appeared. I would then explain that when the Holy Spirit comes upon them and fills them, it's a good thing, but if there is anything not so good in there that needs to come out, it may feel strange. Then I would tell the thing to leave, maybe get the person to breathe in the Holy Spirit and breathe out any evil spirits and they would find the symptoms leave quickly. Once they encounter Jesus like this, through His Holy Spirit, the person often asks what they are experiencing, and then wants to know Him more. I explain who Jesus is and what He did for them and ask them if they know Him. Usually they say they don't know Him personally, or they know a bit about Him, so I ask if they would like to really know Him. I then explain how He gave His life for them, and ask if they would like to give their life to Him. They normally say they would like to, so I help them to pray out loud and talk to Jesus and explain that He will come into their lives by His Holy Spirit when they invite Him.

Ministering in the Holy Spirit

Increasingly you will find that as you introduce people to Jesus and they become filled with His Holy Spirit, they begin to shake or find it difficult to stand. It is important not to quench the Holy Spirit but let Him do a deep work in them and release joy and peace in their lives, but we also need to learn how to be full of the Holy Spirit and carry the anointing without it preventing us from functioning. As you pray for others, you will often experience what I describe as a 'back draught' of the Holy Spirit and sometimes I can hardly stand. However, as tempting as it may be to fall under this power I may be in the supermarket or working in our shop so it's important to be able to carry on with what I'm doing at the same time. We need to learn how to steward the anointing, how to carry the glory without falling over and laughing hysterically. "The spirit of the prophet is subject to the prophet" (1 Corinthians 14:32).

But at other times the Lord wants to do a work in us and it's important to be able to let go and let Him do it. I remember hearing about Heidi Baker, the wonderful missionary in Mozambique. She and her husband Rolland had moved to that African nation as missionaries, but were struggling to lead people to Jesus and establish churches. One day she attended a conference in Toronto. She was whacked by the Holy Spirit and appeared drunk for a number of days, so much so, that she needed to be pushed around in a wheelchair. In this state she must have appeared crazy, but during that time God did such an amazing work in her heart that since she and her husband went back to Mozambique, they have planted out hundreds of thousands of churches, seen numerous miracles and children raised from the dead.

"So I say walk by the Spirit, and you will not gratify the desires of the sinful nature… but if you are led by the Spirit, you are not under the law… Since we live by the Spirit let us keep in step with the Spirit" (Galatians 5:16-25).

Chapter Four

Supernatural Knowledge

"O Lord, open our eyes so we may see"

The first time I can remember operating in supernatural knowledge was in the early Eighties when I was fifteen or sixteen years of age. I had spent the afternoon in town with my friends and was riding home on the bus, a ten minute journey. It was a Saturday afternoon and the bus was crammed full of people. The only places left were two seats near the front, and I sat on one of these, next to the window and an elderly lady came and filled the other.

I remember staring blankly out of the window, thinking of nothing in particular as the bus wound its way through the crowded streets. In a few minutes I would be home. Just then a thought came into my head; "Should I talk to the woman sitting next to me about Jesus?" What a strange thought! I wondered what had made me think that. Then I realised it must be the Holy Spirit speaking to me. I was a shy teenager, the bus was packed and that would be the last thing I would want to do!

Looking out of the window, I silently made a deal with the Lord, "I will speak to her about You, if You give me something to say to her." I secretly hoped that would be the end of it, and knew that my stop would be coming up soon and the pressure would be off. However another thought leaped into my consciousness, "She has a daughter who is seriously ill with stomach problems." I had no way out! I had made a deal with the Lord and couldn't back out now. A little bit of pride in me died that day. I was so embarrassed.

I looked at the woman to my right. She seemed very old to me. I plucked up some courage and reluctantly spoke to her, "Excuse me, I'm a Christian and I think Jesus just told me something about you." All eyes turned to me as the rest of the crowded bus was silent, apart from the humming of the engine. The old lady looked at me and, fiddling with her hearing aid retorted, "Eh?" My heart sank. I realised she was quite deaf. I took a deep breath and repeated my statement, this time much louder, sensing my face burning with redness as I was aware of many other people hanging on every word I uttered! "Oh Lord," I thought, "I can't believe I'm doing this. I feel like some sort of Jesus freak."

This time the woman heard me. She was interested to know what God had to say. I asked her if she had a daughter who was ill with stomach problems. She looked surprised and told me she was on her way to visit her daughter in hospital, seriously ill with stomach complications and she seemed agitated. I remember putting my hand on hers to comfort her and told her that God loved her. I thought, "Why would God tell me that her daughter is ill without doing something about it?" So I took a step of faith and said, "I think God wants to heal your daughter. Can I pray?"

This teenage girl, full of self-doubt and shy misgivings, became a vessel by which the Lord could demonstrate His love and power. However, I was aware that my stop was coming up next, so I prayed and asked God to heal her daughter, and for the woman to be filled with His peace, and then I apologised for having to dash and up I got, said a quick goodbye and fled from the bus, glad to be away from the humiliation.

Once I had calmed down I realised that something remarkable had happened. God had given me information about a person I didn't know, I had spoken it out and it was accurate. I knew I wouldn't see that woman again and I wouldn't know if her daughter was healed, but I had been obedient to the Holy Spirit. That was what mattered.

Words of Knowledge

1 Corinthians 12:4-11 lists nine gifts that are given to us from the Holy Spirit. One of these gifts is described by the Apostle Paul as a "word of knowledge" (see verse 8). A word of knowledge is when someone is given information from the Holy Spirit

about something that they would not naturally know, like the example of the lady on the bus. We can also operate in the Spirit of Knowledge which is listed in Isaiah 11:2. The Holy Spirit knows what is going on in heaven and speaks it to us.

You can operate in the gifts of the Spirit without knowing what they are, but Paul said "Now concerning spiritual gifts, brothers, I do not want you to be unaware" (1 Corinthians 12:1).

Jesus stated "I tell you the truth, the Son can do nothing by himself; he can do only what he sees his Father doing, because whatever the Father does the Son also does" (John 5:19) and "By myself I can do nothing" (John 5:30). We are to live like that too. Jesus said, "...Peace be with you! As the Father has sent me, I am sending you" (John 20:21).

The Holy Spirit will speak only what He hears and will make known to us what the Father is doing in heaven. "But when he, the Spirit of truth comes, he will guide you into all truth. He will not speak on his own; he will speak only what he hears, and he will tell you what is yet to come" (John 16:13).

Hearing the Voice of the Holy Spirit

The Holy Spirit speaks in many ways. When Jesus was on the earth He often spoke in parables and He gives revelation that requires us to ask Him to help interpret. Below are just a few of the ways the Holy Spirit speaks to us. I have taken examples from some of my past experiences. It can be helpful to learn from other people's experiences and mistakes.

A Thought

A number of years ago I was walking my son Phoenix to school. As we entered the school gate, a young woman walked in front of us with her son. I noticed her skirt and remember thinking how nice it was. I didn't think much more than that.

The next morning I awoke early and my first thought was of the woman's skirt. I wondered why that was on my mind so I asked the Holy Spirit if there was a particular reason. I began to feel emotional and realised the Lord wanted me to pray for her. So I began to pray and even though I asked the Lord what He wanted me to say, all I sensed was that I needed to talk to her.

I took Phoenix to school that morning in plenty of time, praying that I would see her. She was nowhere to be seen, so I waited a while and then spotted her arriving late. After she had dropped off her son I approached her, feeling nervous. I had not spoken to her before and wasn't exactly sure what I should say. The Lord had still not given me anything to say to her. But I knew He had highlighted her to me for a reason.

I said "hello" and told her my name. I said I was a Christian and that God had a message for her. I still didn't know what the message was, but I stepped out in faith, hoping the Lord would reveal something to me. Then it happened. As I began to speak, the words seemed to flow out of me, inspired by the Holy Spirit. I was so thankful!

I explained, "You are in a desperate situation, something connected with your family. You are not sure if you believe in God, but you have been crying out to Him and asking Him to help you. I am here to tell you that God has heard your cries and He has sent me to tell you that He is going to do a miracle in your life. You haven't been sleeping and you don't know where to turn. If you give your life to Jesus and follow Him, He will turn your life around and answer your prayers within two weeks!"

As I said it, I was hoping I was right! But as I looked at her, I saw tears flowing down her cheeks and she was nodding. She said everything I'd told her was true. In fact she was so concerned, she was taking tranquilisers but they weren't helping. The problem had been going on for two years.

I explained to her about Jesus; the fact that He had died in her place, He had taken her sin and disease upon Him and how she could have a new life because He had risen from the dead and sent His Holy Spirit. She was enthralled and readily let me pray with her and took a leaflet on knowing Jesus that I carried in my bag.

A few days later I saw her again and she told me that she had given her life to Jesus and already she was feeling better and had stopped taking the tranquilisers. I prayed with her again and the next time I saw her, two weeks later, she excitedly explained that her life had turned around, the family situation was resolved and she would not now lose her home. Her husband was a Muslim and I was able to prophesy to him too.

A Feeling or an Emotion

An example of this would be the story I told about the stillborn baby and the woman at the checkout.

A Sensation

A number of years ago I awoke early one Sunday morning. I asked the Lord what He wanted to do that morning in the church that I attended at the time. The word 'Salvation' entered my mind. I smiled, knowing that someone would get saved that morning. But I wanted to know more details about that person, so I asked the Holy Spirit to be specific. Instantly my left knee began to tingle. I wondered if it was someone who had injured their knee.

After the worship time in the meeting that morning, one of the Elders got up to speak and his subject was 'Salvation'. I was pleased I'd heard right, but I knew there was someone specific the Lord wanted to communicate with. Towards the end of the preaching, I began to ask the Holy Spirit if I should share a word of knowledge about a painful left knee. However, as I sat there, my mind began to wander. I remembered some years previously how the Lord had given me the first names of a visiting couple to the church and how I had described their circumstances and their names and how they, and an onlooker had rushed to the front and given their lives to Jesus as a result.

At first I thought my mind was wandering, but then I began to wonder why I was remembering that incident. I realised the Holy Spirit could be speaking to me, at which point the Elder wrapped up his talk. I decided to step out in faith and stood in front of the 300 or so members of the congregation and began to speak, "I sense the Holy Spirit showing me there is a person here this morning that doesn't yet know Jesus. You haven't been here before and you're not sure what you're doing here. But God has been speaking to you through the message this morning and He is telling you that He loves you and that 'today is the day of your salvation'. I believe your name begins with 'nee'."

I looked around and invited that person to come forward, but no-one moved. I felt my face begin to turn pink as I realised no-one was responding and I had just given a specific word of knowledge. Maybe I should have played it safe, perhaps I should have told everyone to close their eyes and bow their heads! But I was just doing what I felt I should do. Nobody came to my aid. The meeting just came to a close and I felt stupid.

A couple of minutes later when people were beginning to disperse, a young guy came up to me, visibly shaken. With his body trembling, he told me that he felt sick. He explained, "When you got up and began to describe a certain person, you were speaking about me. I began to shake and thought I was going to throw up. I tried to tell myself that you couldn't know about me, that God isn't real. But then you said my name began with 'nee' and I knew without a doubt that it was me. I am extremely cynical and wouldn't normally believe any of this stuff. But my name is 'Nino'.

A Person's Appearance

One morning I asked the Holy Spirit to show me something I was going to do that day and I began to picture someone I knew who was a nurse. She would wear a navy blue top and trousers at work. An hour or two later I saw a woman who was wearing a navy top and trousers, although it was not a uniform. I began to prophesy to her and an image of my friend came to mind; this friend had set up a pregnancy crisis centre to help women make choices other than abortion. So I prophesied to the lady that she would work with women who were pregnant and set up a pregnancy crisis centre. I then suddenly thought of someone else I knew that was writing a book so I prophesied to the woman that she'd write. She laughed and told me that she was about to set up a pregnancy crisis centre, actually a home for girls who didn't have abortions. She said she was about to start writing, but had asked the Lord for confirmation before she launched out! All I had was an image of these people in my mind and I took a step of faith and spoke it out. I realise the Lord must have been speaking to me so many times in the past, but I never knew! I thought it was just my mind wandering.

A Vision

"Has anyone here had an incident with a squirrel?" I was the after dinner speaker at a hotel a couple of years ago. Before I set off that evening, I'd asked the Holy Spirit to give me some words of knowledge. One that I received was an inner vision. I had my eyes closed but I saw the vision clearly, much as you would in a dream. I saw a squirrel running and a person falling. After I'd asked the question that evening to a group of people, I was surprised to see a lady raise her hand and come out to where I was standing with the microphone. She explained that some months previously, she'd been walking along the pavement when she tripped and fell and saw a squirrel running away. She realised she must have tripped over the squirrel, but she blacked out and had experienced similar blackouts over the past few months since the episode with the squirrel. I explained that it was probably an evil spirit that was causing the blackouts. We broke off any curse and told any evil spirits to leave, she felt something go as we prayed.

The squirrel I had seen was with my minds eye while my physical eyes were closed. Sometimes we see into the spiritual realm with our eyes open and we can actually see something that others cannot see. The difference between these two ways of seeing is referred to as an outer vision or an inner vision. I often have outer visions where I see with my eyes open. This will be only for a few seconds, just enough for me to ask the Holy Spirit to help me understand what I've just seen. Once I saw a huge pentagram outside a shop, this was only for a few seconds, but the Lord was telling me there was occult activity going on in that place.

A Dream

One night I dreamed that I was on a bus and met a woman who told me her name. She had a large pentagram around her neck and in the dream I was praying for her eye and her back, both of which were healed. The next day my husband and I walked into a shop which we realised was selling new age/occult items. Then we noticed that the woman from the dream was standing behind the shop counter! She was the owner. I told her I had dreamed about her the night before and asked if she had problems with her eye and back. She did, so we prayed and she felt the power of Jesus going through her. Her name was related to the name in my dream.

Sharing the Supernatural Knowledge

It is one thing to receive the knowledge, but it's another to understand what it is you've received and subsequently know what to do with it. We need wisdom. I am never completely sure of the interpretation I receive, but this is where faith comes in! The Bible says it's impossible to please God without faith (see Hebrews 11:6). He loves it when we step out and take a risk in the hope that maybe it could be God, with a heart to please Him and share His love. It provides a wonderful opportunity for a miracle. I find that even if what I'm saying is not quite accurate, the person I'm speaking to is so pleased to have someone trying to encourage them that they don't seem to mind. God is more interested in our motives than our accuracy.

It's important to be humble, be loving towards people and share things in a way that will strengthen, encourage or comfort them (see 1 Corinthians 14:3). I remember once when we were at MorningStar School of Ministry, one of the students sensed from the Holy Spirit that a lady at the bus stop was unable to have children. Unfortunately he didn't choose his words carefully. He approached her and enquired, "Do you have any children?" She answered, "No" so he continued, "Would you like one?" She glared at him with a disgusted look on her face and he walked off feeling rather embarrassed. He was given full marks though for trying!

Think laterally. The interpretation is not always as you would assume. At a conference the Lord once gave me the words, "Licence to Kill, like James Bond, 007". I imagined it to be for a secret agent, but it was actually for a guy who had a licence plate on his car ending with 007 and the Lord was calling him to be His secret agent in the spiritual realm.

The Purpose of Supernatural Knowledge

The Lord reveals information about a person in order to lead them to Jesus or to bring about God's purpose in their life. Remember in John 1 when Nathanael met Jesus who revealed to him that He had seen him sitting under the fig tree? Jesus had seen him in the Spirit and because of this, Nathanael believed that Jesus was the Son of God.

In the fourth chapter of John, Jesus supernaturally knew that the woman He had just met at the well had been married five times and the man she was currently living with was not her husband. She realised He was the Messiah and proceeded to evangelise her town. What a result from a word of knowledge!!

It is interesting to note that in the examples I've cited Jesus shares supernatural knowledge about unbelievers in everyday life situations. It led to their salvation.

Generally, people initially seem disinterested in Jesus if they don't already know him. However, tell them something about themselves that you could not naturally know, or demonstrate the power of Jesus with a miracle, suddenly you have their attention and they want to know more about Him.

Supernatural knowledge carries power as it is spoken. "But if an unbeliever or someone who does not understand comes in while everybody is prophesying, he will be convinced by all that he is a sinner and will be judged by all, and the secrets of his heart will be laid bare. So he will fall down and worship God, exclaiming, "God is really among you!" (1 Corinthians 14:24,25).

Earnestly Desire the Spiritual Gifts

1 Corinthians 14:1 exhorts us to earnestly desire supernatural gifts, especially the gift of prophecy, one of the revelatory gifts. Often times I've heard people say we should seek the Giver, not the gifts, but that does not line up with Scripture. Of course, we should seek after the Lord with all our hearts, but we are also exhorted to seek after the gifts passionately.

I described earlier in this chapter how I operated in the word of knowledge as a teenager on a bus. A similar incident occurred again soon afterwards, but I didn't continue to pursue the gift and it was ten or twelve years later before I operated in the supernatural gifts again. I was sitting in a church service and the person preaching asked the congregation to think of a time in their lives when they were most fulfilled. Despite being happily married with two children, and a good career, my mind went back to the time I was on the bus, ministering to a woman with a word of knowledge, and other times when I was sharing the gospel with my friends and on the streets. I realised that was what I was born to do. So I began to ask the Lord to give me supernatural knowledge again. I prayed earnestly for two years but nothing seemed to happen.

However, one Sunday morning I awoke early, feeling such a heavy presence of the Holy Spirit I couldn't move! So many thoughts were rushing through my head, I couldn't understand them - thoughts of earthquakes, people screaming, an army rising up, people falling on their knees and praying and the righteous shining. I managed to climb out of bed and sat at my computer. I typed as the words flowed and realised I had typed two pages. It was a clear prophetic word for the church. He had given me much more than I had asked for. At the end of the prophecy were around eight words of knowledge for specific people, all beginning with the person's name whom I didn't know! I shared the word that morning in the meeting and the presence of the Fear of the Lord was tangible as the whole congregation knelt and all eight people responded to the words of knowledge.

Jesus explained that He only did what He saw the Father doing in Heaven and that as the Father sent Him, so He sends us. We must learn to see what takes place in Heaven, in the supernatural realm, in order for us to bring Heaven to earth. That is what we are called to do. Our eyes can be opened to the supernatural realm, just like Elisha's servant Gehazi. He was terrified by the sight of the surrounding enemy army until Elisha asked the Lord to open his eyes to see in the supernatural realm. He then saw that the heavenly host around them, far outnumbered the enemy chariots surrounding them (see 2 Kings 6:17).

Many times when the Lord speaks we imagine it is our own thoughts or we're not brave enough to speak it out. You will find that if you do step out in obedient faith and share what you have received, it will almost always bear good fruit. If your heart is right before the Lord and you are reaching out to people in love, the worst that can happen is that you grow in humility. And surely that can't be a bad thing, can it!?

Chapter Five

Power of the Spoken Word

"Declare a thing and it will be established for you"

My husband Rob and I were given some money so that we could go away and have some time out. It just so happened that the previous week, four people within five days had prophesied to me about St Cuthbert. I didn't know much about this early mystic but I knew that he had been based at Lindisfarne for much of his life, a small island off the coast of Northumberland, North East England. It is also known as 'Holy Island' and is still a place of pilgrimage.

I wondered if we could stay on the island for a week at short notice, but I'd been told there were only a few houses available to rent on the island. Apparently they were expensive and availability was limited; bookings were normally taken a year in advance. We wanted to go virtually the next day! However I did a search on the internet and came up with a lovely cottage right in the middle of Lindisfarne that had a cancellation and was available for the week we wanted to go. Surprisingly, it was half the normal rate, so we quickly booked it.

I checked the weather forecast and it was about as bad as it could be in an English summer: heavy rain and howling winds all week, with no let up. "Well at least we can watch movies and eat lots of good food," we consoled ourselves. On the journey up there, the weather was just as the forecast predicted; we could barely see out of the windscreen despite the wipers being on full power. As we were leaving the main road and turning to approach the island, there was a huge lightning bolt that appeared to be straight in front of the car, together with a loud crash of thunder. "Welcome to Lindisfarne" we exclaimed.

We unpacked our belongings in the pretty cottage and went for a short walk to the sea with our hoods pulled tightly around our heads, unable to see much in front of us. With my hands raised, I stood on the cliff edge and declared, "I take authority over the storm clouds and I command them to move away in the name of Jesus. Sunshine come out and rain stay away until the day we leave." Rob smiled. As we walked back to the cottage we realised the rain had stopped and the clouds were moving away. For the whole week we had glorious sunshine, we spent most of the time outside, walking the island, receiving strategy from the Lord and relaxing by the sea, reading about St Cuthbert. The day we left, the heavens opened and the weather was exactly as it was the day we arrived. When we spoke to people back in Chester they told us the weather had been atrocious all week, it appeared to be only the North East that had experienced no rain!

St Cuthbert

St Cuthbert lived in the Seventh Century and was an early mystic and miracle worker. He performed so many miracles of healing that he was known as the 'Wonder worker of Britain' and people came from far and wide for miracles and to glean his wisdom on spiritual matters. St Cuthbert moved in great spiritual authority over the weather, birds and animals. One day whilst walking for miles with a young monk on a missionary journey, Cuthbert told the young man to look up at an eagle flying overhead and asked him if it was possible for God to feed them by way of the eagle. Just then the eagle swooped to a river close by and presented them with a large fish. Cuthbert cut the fish and gave half of it to the eagle. St Bede wrote of his preaching that "Cuthbert had such a light in his angelic face, and such a love for proclaiming his Good News, that none hid their innermost secrets from him." According to Bede (673-735 AD), Cuthbert's body remained uncorrupted years after his death. In fact there is even an account from as late as 1540 of his body discovered in Henry VIII's reign "lying whole uncorrupt with his face bare, and his beard as of a fortnight's growth" (see www.dur.ac.uk).

In Scripture we read the prophet Jeremiah's account of how the Lord showed him the power of the spoken word. "Then the LORD reached out his hand and touched my mouth and said to me, "Now, I have put my words in your mouth. See, today I appoint you over nations and kingdoms to uproot and tear down, to destroy and overthrow, to build and to plant" (Jeremiah 1:9,10). We can use words for building and planting and for rooting up and pulling down those things which are against God's plans.

The Power of the Tongue

Words are powerful; more powerful than we realise. Some years ago, I had set up a business and a guy called me and said he was a potential customer. I was happy to answer his questions as I mistakenly thought he was a client, but he had in fact lied to me. He was a competitor, attempting to glean information about my business. One of my employees was not a Christian, but the next day I arrived at the office and told her that despite the fact that he had lied to me and tried to take advantage, I had forgiven him. I prayed and asked God to deal with him. I read a Psalm and quoted something like, "My enemies turn back; they stumble and perish before you" (Psalm 9:3). I explained to my non-Christian colleague that we did not need to worry about that guy any more.

Later that day I received a phone call from one of my suppliers. Towards the end of the conversation, he asked if I'd heard the news about another of his customers. He told me that the guy who had called me pretending to be a customer had been involved in a car crash that morning, and that he and his business partner had been killed instantly. I was shocked. I could not deny that there was a compelling connection between what I had so recently said and what had come about. My non-Christian colleague was taken aback and needless to say, she told me she would never get on the wrong side of me and was always going to remain my friend!!

Now as far as I know, I did not curse that guy or say anything I should not have said. I had forgiven him and let it go. Yet he died very quickly after I prayed. We need to be careful what we speak out. The Bible says that "The tongue has the power of life and death" (Proverbs 18:21).

One day, I was in a small meeting of leaders and one of the group was talking about his life and the fact that he "was a failure" in a particular area. I was surprised at what he had said. Later, at home, I could not get those words out of my head and felt that he was speaking out the enemy's thoughts and had come into agreement with him. I was sorry that I had not realised earlier when I had chance to speak to him. The next day I decided I should contact him but was shocked to learn that he had been rushed into hospital with 'heart failure'. It is tragic that the word 'failure' he had spoken out the night before, had manifested in his heart the next morning as he came into agreement with the enemy.

People often unconsciously do this. How many times have you heard someone say, "I'm worried to death," or "I'm sick and tired?" It is important to speak out God's plan for our lives and for others, not the enemy's plan. We must not criticise or speak negative words about ourselves or other people. How can we be trusted with the power to raise the dead if we criticise and speak destructive things about others or indeed about ourselves?

We can learn from Jesus' reaction when a negative word was spoken to him in Matthew 16:23. Jesus had been telling His disciples that He would die and be raised to life after three days.

Peter mistakenly spoke out words which he no doubt saw as loyal and honouring to Jesus when he said, "Never, Lord! This shall never happen to you!" Jesus' response was severe, "Get behind me, Satan! You are a stumbling block to me; you do not have in mind the things of God, but the things of men." We see that even a close disciple of Jesus spoke out words that were from the enemy and against the Father's will, but instantly Jesus rebuked Satan. Each time someone says something to you that is contrary to God's plan for your life, you can speak back and stop those words from impacting you.

A number of years ago in one of our meetings, I was teaching on understanding our purpose and destiny. One of the activations I used was to consider with the Holy Spirit the things you would like to have achieved by the end of your earthly life. I gave an example by reading out some of the things I was going to do in my lifetime. Someone laughingly shouted out, "You'll be dead by the time you're...(and then said an age)." Smiling, I instantly counteracted it by saying, "I rebuke that in the name of Jesus," but afterwards I realised that I was rebuking the devil's plan for my life and I could easily have taken that on board and begun to agree with it. It was a demon manifesting through that person. I am sure that could have turned out to be true if I had not cancelled it by the power of Jesus as soon as that curse was spoken. It is so easy to say things thoughtlessly but it is important for us to learn to guard our tongues.

Lying to the Holy Spirit

The story of Ananias and Sapphira in the fifth chapter of Acts intrigues me. "Now a man named Ananias, together with his wife Sapphira, also sold a piece of property. With his wife's full knowledge he kept back part of the money for himself, but brought the rest and put it at the apostles' feet. Then Peter said, "Ananias, how is it that Satan has so filled your heart that you have lied to the Holy Spirit and have kept for yourself some of the money you received for the land? Didn't it belong to you before it was sold? And after it was sold, wasn't the money at your disposal? What made you think of doing such a thing? You have not lied to men but to God." When Ananias heard this, he fell down and died. And great fear seized all who heard what had happened. Then the young men came forward, wrapped up his body, and carried him out and buried him.

About three hours later his wife came in, not knowing what had happened. Peter asked her, "Tell me, is this the price you and Ananias got for the land?" "Yes," she said, "that is the price." Peter said to her, "How could you agree to test the Spirit of the Lord? Look! The feet of the men who buried your husband are at the door, and they will carry you out also." At that moment she fell down at his feet and died. Then the young men came in and, finding her dead, carried her out and buried her beside her husband. Great fear seized the whole church and all who heard about these events." Well, I'm not surprised they were full of fear! Imagine if that happened in your church?

The fact is, this couple lied to the Holy Spirit. They didn't have to give any of the money to the apostles. They could have kept it all. But because they lied to the Holy Spirit, saying that the money they were giving was all of it, but actually having kept some for themselves, it resulted in fatal consequences. The love of money is the root of all evil. You cannot serve God and money. The economy is being shaken. The Lord will continue to do this until He returns. He is interested in our heart's desire and what we hold dear to us. I believe many Christians in these end times will be full of fear and will ultimately lose their lives because of the choices they make with regard to money. Follow the Lord with all your heart and don't be ruled by money, don't make decisions based on finances.

I remember Robin McMillan, (Pastor at MorningStar Ministries in South Carolina when Rob and I were there) commenting that people should be scared to go to church and scared not to. I believe we will again see this happening as we begin to move in supernatural power, as we speak out under the anointing of the Holy Spirit, to build, plant, uproot and overthrow.

At one of our Friday night meetings a gang of teenagers came in. After we prophesied over them, many gave their lives to Jesus. But a visitor at the meeting who had been a Christian many years began to pass notes to them and was trying to distract them with false doctrines. I realised he was demonised and managed to put a stop to it in the meeting, but I was concerned and didn't want it to happen again the following week. So I chatted to the Lord about it and I asked the Lord to set this man free. I said if He wanted to use us to help him get free, that would be OK, and I remember asking the Lord not to allow him back to the meeting unless he was free. The following week at the same time we were in our meeting, that guy dropped down dead as he was walking along the street. His heart stopped. I don't think there was any pre-known medical reason for this. Words are powerful.

Curses and Blessings

A friend of mine related a story to me of how she discovered the power of words, even before she became a Christian. She began, "I remember being in agony with my back. It was going into spasms and I could not take pain killers or have an x-ray because I was pregnant. My husband said it was all in my head and was laughing. Later, I told his sister about it. I said I hope he has something really bad like piles and no one believes him. Well, about five years later he started to have a problem. He was worried sick with it and kept going back to the doctors and trying different meds and different diets. He was scared to eat and thought he must have bowel cancer. No one could understand the drama he was causing. After months of trying different things he eventually caught an emergency flight back to his home country, worried sick. It cost a fortune. They even gave him a full row of seats so he could lie down to make him more comfortable.

He went straight from the airport to accident and emergency at hospital. They admitted him, gave him intrusive camera investigations and an operation to try and find out the source of the problem. He was so worried, especially as the other patients on his ward had severe diagnoses with cancer and the like. However it just turned out to be a bad case of haemorrhoids. He had to spend several weeks in his home country before he found out all was clear. After I became a Christian and learned about the power of the spoken word I realised that I had caused my husband's suffering just by my words. Of course I had no idea I was putting a curse on him at the time and am very careful now in what I speak over people."

We can curse or bless with the words we speak. Earlier today I popped into our shop, 'Spirit,' in

Chester for a meeting with someone. A psychic medium came in and we got chatting. I noticed she had hearing aids in her ears so I asked if she would like me to pray. She replied that she says her own prayers; she's involved with reiki and spirit guides. I suggested that perhaps the reiki wasn't working as she was obviously hard of hearing and explained to her the difference between the power of the Holy Spirit through Jesus Christ and other powers which are evil spirits.

My hand began to hurt so I asked if she had a problem with her hand. She told me she had arthritis in both hands and was in constant pain. She opened out her hands and I held them and began to pray. I took authority over the arthritis and told it to leave in the name of Jesus. She said all the pain left, so I asked if I could pray for her ears too. She turned off her hearing aids, I put my hands on her ears and told the deaf spirit to leave. It must have left straight away as she said her hearing was better. She could hear people talking at the other end of the shop.

Suddenly she reached out her hand to touch my neck and tried to get a word of knowledge for me, although I knew it wasn't through the Holy Spirit. She seemed to think I had pain and told me where it was, but I said, "No, I have no pain at all. Maybe what you are sensing is the enemy's plan for me, so I take authority over the words you have just spoken and break them off me in the name of Jesus and by the blood of Jesus." I said it with a smile and she didn't seem offended. Instead she took a booklet about Jesus and said she was looking forward to reading it when she arrived home.

Controlling the Tongue

We can curse people by the words we use. "You'll never come to any good," "You stupid girl" or other such phrases that easily come out of our mouths, can actually affect those people for the rest of their lives. It is also easy to curse oneself with phrases such as, "I'm sick and tired," "I'll always be fat" or "I'm scared to death." Make a decision not to do this anymore.

In these times, I believe we will see an increase in power as we create and uproot by the words we proclaim. Consider the fig tree that Jesus encountered in Matthew 21. It was not bearing fruit so He spoke to it and told it never to bear fruit again. By the next day the fig tree had withered from the roots and died. Jesus went on to explain to the disciples, "...if you have faith and do not doubt, not only can you do what was done to the fig tree, but also you can say to this mountain, 'Go, throw yourself into the sea,' and it will be done." That level of supernatural power is available to us as we submit to Jesus and speak out in faith.

Can God trust us?

Is God able to trust us? We have authority and power in the tongue to "give life to the dead and call things that are not as though they are" (Romans 4:17). Perhaps the Lord is waiting for us to mature in the way we speak before He releases creative miracles through our proclamations. Let us try and follow Jesus' example: Jesus said, "So whatever I say is just what the Father has told me to say" (John 12:50). Wow! Imagine if we only spoke what we heard the Father say through the Holy Spirit.

James, the brother of Jesus also understood the power of the spoken word, "Likewise the tongue is a small part of the body, but it makes great boasts. Consider what a great forest is set on fire by a small spark. The tongue also is a fire, a world of evil among the parts of the body. It corrupts the whole person, sets the whole course of his life on fire, and is itself set on fire by hell. All kinds of animals, birds, reptiles and creatures of the sea are being tamed and have been tamed by man, but no man can tame the tongue. It is a restless evil, full of deadly poison. With the tongue we praise our Lord and Father, and with it we curse men, who have been made in God's likeness. Out of the same mouth come praise and cursing. My brothers, this should not be" (James 3:5-10). King Solomon also understood the power of the spoken word: "With his mouth the godless destroys his neighbour" (Proverbs 11:9).

And here a Psalm of David: "Lord, who may dwell in your sanctuary? Who may live on your holy hill? He whose walk is blameless and who does what is righteous, who speaks the truth from his heart and has no slander on his tongue" (Psalm 15:1-3).

Finally, let's look at an occasion when Jesus spoke on the topic, "Out of the overflow of the heart the mouth speaks… I tell you that men will have to give account on the day of judgment for every careless word they have spoken. For by your words you will be acquitted and by your words you will be condemned" (Matthew 12:34-37). You should be getting the point by now!! So let's consider some ways in which we can build one another up, give life to the dead and create by calling things that are not as though they are (see Romans 4:17).

Speak out in Faith

A number of years ago we were prayer walking around our community and asking the Lord to give us a building from which we could open a miracle café. We saw a building and felt the Lord say we could have the use of it, despite the fact that the local council who owned the shops had already told me there was a long waiting list for those premises. Apparently we were at the bottom of that list. The following Sunday morning I took the microphone in our church meeting and thanked the Lord that He was going to give us that building rent free. A few people were surprised as we had been told there was no chance we would be able to get it, even if we paid. The next day I was invited to a meeting where the people who were renting the premises asked if we would like to rent that shop instead of them. I smiled and nodded and then they said that we could have it rent free. God will back you up as you step out in faith and declare things that are not as though they are.

Remember when Elijah said to Ahab, "As the Lord God of Israel lives, whom I serve, there will be neither dew nor rain for the next few years except at my word" (1 Kings 17:1)? Elijah was operating under the Old Covenant. Through Jesus we now have greater power than Elijah did. In so many words, Elijah was saying, 'In the name of Jesus I declare it is not going to rain until I tell it to rain.'

I have practiced stopping the rain on a number of occasions. I already mentioned what happened when we went to Lindisfarne. Other times have included moving house, outdoor baptisms, important outdoor birthday parties and so on. It has worked each time, but I don't do it often. In our previous house we had stubborn weeds in the garden that wouldn't go no matter how much weed killer we used and how often we tried to dig them up. I decided one day to speak to them so I cursed them like Jesus cursed the fig tree and the next day they were covered in white spots and began to shrivel up.

As we practice these things it will stand us in good stead for when we need to demonstrate the power of God when facing such situations as Elijah did on Mount Carmel with the prophets of Baal and as Moses did when in a power demonstration with Pharaoh and his evil magicians. It is interesting that both Moses and Elijah appeared to the disciples with

Jesus on the Mount of Transfiguration (see Matthew 17). As we walk in spiritual authority and the glory of Jesus, God will validate what we speak as He did with these great men of faith.

Speaking Healing and Blessing

Speaking healing and blessing is powerful. Miracles can be brought about by our declarations. God created the heavens and the earth by speaking. Often when I pray for someone who needs a new body part, I will say, "I speak a creative miracle, we release a brand new kidney from heaven in Jesus name" and instantly the person will be healed.

A Centurion understood how Jesus could speak the word and his servant would be healed, without Jesus even having to visit him in person (see Matthew 8:5-13). You can speak a word and people will be healed even if you are on the other side of the world.

A friend of mine phoned me one day to say she had been in bed for two weeks with two trapped discs in her back. She was experiencing a lot of pain and wanted me to pray for her. I prayed over the phone and then after the phone call ended, I imagined going into her house and up into her bedroom where she was sitting on her bed. I placed my hands on her back as though I was there in the room with her. I commanded the discs to move back into place and for the pain to leave in the name of Jesus; I said this out loud. Also in the Spirit I saw oil flowing over her head and down her back. Soon afterwards she excitedly called me back. She'd had a vision where I had appeared in her room, placed my hands on her back and spoke to the discs in her back to be healed. She then felt oil being poured over her head, down her back and she jumped up completely healed and pain free! It's great being able to affect people in other places without even having to leave your home!

Practical Application

Think about the times you have spoken negative words to others, either to their faces or behind their backs. It's a good idea to speak out loud and confess to the Lord what you have said, and ask Him to forgive you. This He will do straight away. Also tell Him of the times you've spoken negatively about yourself and ask Him to forgive you for this too. Then repent from believing words that others have spoken over you.

When you believe what someone says about you, it empowers the words that have been spoken, they impact your life and what has been prophesied comes into being, whether good or bad. Renounce the curses and the evil spirits that have become attached to you and to others through what has been spoken, sever the power of those words by the blood of Jesus and speak blessing and destiny over them and yourself. The overcomers in Revelation overcame Satan and his accusations by the blood of the Lamb and the word of their testimony (see Revelation 12:11).

"You will also declare a thing, And it will be established for you; So light will shine on your ways" (Job 22:28 NKJV).

Speak out prophetic words given to you by others and proclaim Scriptures. Declare and decree the purposes of God for you, your family, your community and your nation. It will be established for you and you will walk in the light of the glory of the Lord.

Chapter Six

Demons

"At the name of Jesus every knee shall bow"

As a believer filled with the power and presence of Jesus and walking in His authority, you will begin to notice things happen as you walk down a street or enter a room. People may see you begin to shine, you will find healings happen spontaneously as you walk past, some will be convicted of sin and ask how they can know Jesus, and others will manifest demons.

It is important not to focus on demons. We must have our eyes fixed on Jesus and His Kingdom, "…in order that Satan might not outwit us. For we are not unaware of his schemes" (2 Corinthians 2:11). It is a mistake to completely ignore the enemy or to believe that he does not exist.

I must point out that I am by no means an expert on deliverance. I am learning as much as I can from the Holy Spirit, many times by trial and error. But I hope that by sharing some of my own experiences I can help you learn more quickly than I did.

97

For years I had dreams where I was being chased by terrifying looking creatures. Initially the monsters would be chasing me in buildings and I would try to escape by climbing out of windows or running up or down stairs. I would wake up full of fear and exhausted from trying to escape. After some time I realised that perhaps it was part of my training. I began to ask the Holy Spirit to teach me to fight. My dreams changed. I would run away from the creatures but then something in me would rise up and I would choose to stand my ground. During the dream, I began to turn and face the creatures and before long I was commanding them to leave in the name of Jesus. By the time the dreams came to an end I would be running towards the creatures, telling them to leave in Jesus' name and killing them with a sword.

Once I had recognised that the Lord was using the dreams to teach me the power and authority I had through Jesus, the dreams stopped and I have not had one since. I felt like Neo in the Matrix movie, practising combat in another world.

Ephesians 6:12 states, "For our struggle is not against flesh and blood, but against the rulers, against the authorities, against the powers of this dark world and against the spiritual forces of evil in the heavenly realms."

After some time I decided I would like the Lord to use me to set captives free. I was aware that many people were bound by Satan and had strongholds in their lives, both Christians and non-Christians. I managed to find and read some books on the subject of deliverance. One I would recommend is Derek Prince's "They Shall Expel Demons" and also any books by Neil T Anderson. However, I really wanted to have a go at it myself and I was hoping to find someone who could teach me.

I asked the Lord to show me someone who was casting out demons from whom I could learn, but I could not find anyone. Even some of the leaders of the church I was attending at the time did not believe that a Christian could be demonised. But I knew that sometimes when praying with Christians there was something else operating in their lives that they were unable to break free from.

So I remember at that time asking the Lord to teach me Himself. I said, "Lord, You know how I need to learn how to cast out demons and I can't find anyone who can teach me? Well, I'd like you to teach me and I'd like to start with something obvious. You know, the sort where the person is writhing around on the floor and speaking in a demonic voice and where the demons come out with screams like they did in the Bible, just so I know I'm doing it right!"

I'm sure the Lord must have smiled, but He certainly answered that prayer and it happened very soon.

On the Job Training

Before we had started leading our own church I awoke early one Sunday morning from a startling dream. In the dream I saw a huge ladybird (ladybug) caught in a spider web. An enormous spider began to move towards the ladybird which then turned into a woman's face. The woman was screaming and as I watched, flames of fire formed in a circle around her face and then I awoke. I sat up in bed and realised the Lord wanted to set that woman free from the occult. I sensed it would happen that morning in church and I would be involved.

My son was ill that day so my husband agreed to stay home with him. I told him I would be late back as I would be casting out demons all morning but not to worry. He said "OK" and kissed me goodbye. I was excited as I drove to church with my teenage daughter, explaining to her what was likely to happen that morning. We arrived at church and I spoke to one of the Elders, warning him of what I thought may take place in the meeting. He looked slightly perplexed and explained that he was the only Elder there that day; the others were away. I told him not to worry, everything would be fine!

I looked around the church and tried to spot the woman in my dream but couldn't see her anywhere. However, halfway through the worship, I was aware of a disturbance by the front door, so I went to investigate. Sure enough, there in front of me was the woman from my dream, although her hairstyle was not the same. She was trying to get into the building but was causing a scene. I realised it was just the demons manifesting so I told the ushers on the door that I would take her round the back. I escorted her down the side alleyway and she told me her name. I knew at once that it was not her real name, but probably her Satanist name, and that of a demon.

We walked into the rear hallway of the Church, but because the worship was well underway, she immediately turned to face me and began to run towards the outer door. I spoke to the demons and said, "Stop in the name of Jesus and let her enter the room." She stopped dead in her tracks and turned around. With my hand on her arm I guided her back towards the service and we entered the room. We sat near the door. A couple came to help and began to pray over her in tongues. I said, "I wouldn't do that if I were you; something's going to happen if you do that," but at the same time I was longing for something to happen!

By this time the worship had ended and it was time for the children to go to their groups. They filed passed us and I stood in front of the woman in case she began to manifest. As soon as the children had gone out, I noticed the woman's eyes rolling back into their sockets so all that was visible were the whites of her eyes. At the same time she began to thrash out with her hands and her legs buckled. She fell to the floor as I tried to catch her and landed face up, one hand trying to strangle herself, the other trying to punch me. Her Doc Martin clad feet kicked anything and anyone who came in her way! But I was ready. I had been waiting for a moment like this for a long time.

A friend of ours was preaching that day and his message just so happened to be on Luke 10 where Jesus explains about the authority His followers have over demons and sends His disciples to cast them out. He was preaching it whilst we were doing it, with sound effects too! The congregation were sitting down listening to his sermon and the demonised woman was flat out on the floor at the back with a number of us trying to prevent her attacking herself and anyone else, and demons were screaming as they manifested.

Despite never having done anything like this before, I took control of the situation and said to those helping, "OK, you pray and I'll cast the demons out." Silently I asked the Holy Spirit to give me the name of the first demon that was to come out. Her fist was inches from my face as I tried to prevent her from punching me. Instantly I knew the name of the first demon. It was tattooed across her knuckles. D-E-A-T-H. "Spirit of death," I challenged. As I spoke its name the woman shrieked, her body convulsed and she became stronger. "Come out in the name of Jesus." She wailed and I sensed a demon come up from her belly but get stuck in her throat. It seemed difficult to get it out. I began to react as I did when one of my children was being obstinate when they were young. I would tell them that if they didn't obey me, on the count of three they would receive a smack.

I pointed to the woman's throat and I spoke to the demon, "On the count of three you will come out in the name of Jesus. One... two... three!" And with a loud scream the demon came out. Wow! I realised what power we have as followers of Jesus.

Instantly I knew the name of the next demon and as I spoke it, the woman let out a blood curdling scream and tried to attack those nearby whilst lying on her back. But the demon had to do as it was told and it came out. I noticed that the microphone my friend was using kept cutting out. Demons sometimes affect electrical equipment. Sometimes lights may start flashing as demons are cast out. Often I will tell demons to go to Jesus once they come out and this usually prevents it happening. I have also noticed that the presence of the Holy Spirit can affect electrical equipment too, it isn't only demons! It's like a power surge.

We continued casting out the demons from this woman all afternoon, long after the service had finished. Normally I would show a person how to get free of evil spirits and encourage them to do it themselves, but if the person is severely demonised, as in this case, you may need to speak to the demons, at least initially. We later found out that this woman had been a Satanist for twenty years. She was so demonised that the demons took over and she later couldn't remember anything that had happened. I wanted to get to the point where she could ask Jesus to come into her life, so we continued on.

The Holy Spirit told me the name of all eighty or so demons that we cast out of her that day, except one. She was lying on her back with her eyes closed and someone sitting near her began to flick through a Bible. Her body contorted as a demon in her tried to get as far away as possible from the Bible. I enquired, "I wonder which demon that is?" and it replied using a demonic voice spoken from her mouth, "Satanic Bible." I said, "Thanks for that. Satanic Bible demon, come out in the name of Jesus!" Immediately the demon screamed and came out. Some of the other demons were named after Satanic rituals, many were things I'd never heard of, but the Holy Spirit gave me their names.

After Deliverance

Eventually that day the woman was free enough to ask Jesus to come into her life, but it took a few attempts for her to say the name Jesus. Later that night as I was falling asleep, feeling very tired after a hard day's work, I noticed some dark shadows moving around in the bedroom and sensed an evil presence. I realised they were evil spirits so I told them to leave in the name of Jesus, and of course, they did. My daughter informed me the next morning that she had some demons in her room, but she'd also told them to leave in the name of Jesus and wasn't bothered by them again.

I apologised to her as I had forgotten to tell any demons to leave that were hanging around after we'd finished the deliverance session earlier that day. It's always a good idea to do this. You don't need to be afraid of demons. They really are scared of every child of God who knows that Jesus is living in them.

"But solid food is for the mature, who by constant use have trained themselves to distinguish good from evil" (Hebrews 5:14). We need to train ourselves by learning to obey the Holy Spirit's promptings and stepping out in faith. It's so much fun!

The Gift of Discerning Spirits

In 1 Corinthians 12:8-10, Paul lists the spiritual gifts available to every follower of Jesus. One of these is 'the discerning of spirits', which is also translated as 'distinguishing between spirits'. The word here translated 'spirit' in Greek is 'pneuma' which can mean the human spirit, the Holy Spirit, angels or evil spirits. If we are anointed by the Holy Spirit to "set the captives free" (Isaiah 61/Luke 4), we need to be able to discern which spirit we are facing.

Sometimes it's obvious. A number of years ago, a woman came to visit me. She had been a Christian for twenty or thirty years and was an active member of our previous church. She came round for a coffee and as she was leaving, standing on my doorstep, she began to accuse me of something that was not true. As she was talking, I watched as her head began to shrink, her features contorted and wrinkles appeared on her face and neck, so much so, that she appeared to be well over one hundred years old! I saw all this happen with my eyes, it wasn't a vision, but was actually happening in the physical realm. I felt an evil presence. I'd never seen anything like this before, and didn't know what to do. If it happened now, I would have told it to come out in the name of Jesus, but I was so shocked, all I could say was, "Well it was nice to see you, goodbye" and I was thinking, "Don't call us, we'll call you!" Just then, my husband Rob came back from work, walked past us both, said "hi" and went into the other room.

Eventually I managed to usher her down the steps and into her car before closing the front door and praying around the hallway as I could still feel the evil in the house. Shocked, I walked into the sitting room and remarked, "You should have seen what just happened!" to which Rob replied, "Yeah I saw it all. Never seen anything like that before, but I knew you could handle it so I left you to it." Thanks for that, I thought. Demons can shape shift.

This sort of thing is going to happen more often! Would you know what to do?

Some Manifestations of Evil Spirits

Sometimes when a demon manifests, it isn't so obvious. One day a woman came into our cafe with a friend. Whilst they were waiting for their food, she told us that she had broken her ribs. We prayed, she felt her ribs move back into place, the pain all left and she said she was healed. Her friend had broken her arm, so we prayed for that and the same thing happened. The friend said she wanted to know Jesus, but as their food had just arrived, we said we'd pray with her after they'd eaten.

The first woman was asking a lot of questions about Jesus, and in answer to one of her questions, I said that we have the power to raise the dead. At that, she stood up, her demeanour changed and she began to get angry. She was shouting at me in front of other customers, she grabbed her friend and stormed out, telling passers-by that they mustn't go into our café. I felt humiliated, upset and shaken. Afterwards I realised it was a demon manifesting. What I should have done was to take authority over it, speak to it and either tell it to come out or be quiet in the name of Jesus.

Mostly, I was upset that the woman's friend had not had the opportunity to give her life to Jesus. A few months later, the Lord reminded me of her, so I prayed that she would meet someone who would lead her to Jesus. An hour or so after I prayed, I went to our local supermarket and was amazed to see her standing by the checkout. She told the friend she was with how Jesus had healed her broken arm, and as we stood in the supermarket car park holding hands, they both gave their lives to Jesus!

You may find that demons manifest when you pray for people. I was running an Alpha course years ago (an evangelistic course with a 'relaxed and informal atmosphere') when a backslidden Christian who had recommitted her life to Jesus the previous week, was having prayer to receive the Holy Spirit. She broke out in a sweat, flung her head back and said she was about to throw up. She dashed to the bathroom and we went to see if she was OK. She told us she had never felt so ill in all her life. We explained that it was an evil spirit manifesting. As it was getting late and the rest of the people there were either new or not yet Christians, we opted to bind the demon and passed her onto the pastoral team who could pray with her another time.

Casting Out an Unclean Spirit

When a demon manifests, it seems to be much easier to cast it out. You may feel awkward at first, but if you have time, you can tell the person that an evil spirit is manifesting and that you are about to speak to the demon, not to them. Then in a normal voice, without having to shout, just speak directly to the demon and command it to be quiet or come out, almost as though you are speaking to a naughty child.

I find that people do not seem to be embarrassed about it, they are usually more than happy to get rid of something that's been bothering them for a long time. Non-Christians seem to be particularly open to the fact that they may have an evil spirit affecting them. I've had instances where someone has said they would like to give their life to Jesus, but they have then been unable to speak. Apart from the first time this happened and I didn't do anything, every other time I have spoken directly to the spirit and told it to let the person speak (in the name of Jesus) and instantly they have been able to ask God for forgiveness, thank Jesus for dying on the cross for them, tell the spirit to leave and ask Him to come into their life and fill them with His Holy Spirit.

One time I was chatting to a woman in our café. The previous Sunday she had visited our meeting but told me that the presence of God was so strong she had literally run out of the building and down the road, despite the fact that she used a walker because of her deformed feet! But in the café she said that she wanted to follow Jesus. We invited her to pray out loud but she clutched her head and said she felt confused. I explained it was a spirit of confusion and that she could tell it to leave in the name of Jesus which she did, and then she was able to be born again. We also prayed for her deformed feet and next time we saw her she was completely healed, they were no longer deformed, the pain was gone and she no longer needed her walker or stick. (She also brought her daughter into the café who was instantly healed of a long term back injury).

We have been given authority over all the power of the enemy and that includes evil spirits.

"The 72 returned with joy and said, Lord, even the demons submit to us in your name" (Luke 10:17). In order for us to use the authority that Jesus has given us over the enemy, we must be submitted to the authority of Jesus in our lives.

Jesus says, "I have given you authority to trample on snakes and scorpions and to overcome all the power of the enemy, nothing will harm you. However, do not rejoice that the spirits submit to you but rather rejoice that your names are written in heaven" (Luke 10:19).

The blood of Jesus and the name of Jesus are more powerful than we realise. "You are my King and my God who decrees victories for Jacob. Through you we push back our enemies, through your name we trample our foes" (Psalm 44:4,5) and "They overcame him (the enemy) by the blood of the Lamb and by the word of their testimony" (Revelation 12:11).

Demons often look for a person to inhabit or influence. If they cannot enter a human body, they will sometimes enter an animal. Remember the account of the demonised man in Mark 5? Jesus cast out a legion (many thousands) of demons and he allowed them to enter the pigs that in turn killed themselves by running into the lake.

I remember one time we were praying with a Christian and as the demons were coming out, her dogs in the adjacent room were barking and whining as if there was an intruder in the house. Now when demons are leaving someone I tell them to go to Jesus as they come out.

There is no need to fear demons. "Having disarmed the powers and authorities, he made a public spectacle of them, triumphing over them by the cross" (Colossians 2:15). They have been disarmed by Jesus.

Choose Whom You Will Serve

A number of years ago, three of us were ministering outdoors in a town in America. A group of people gave their lives to Jesus and then were filled with the Holy Spirit and began speaking in tongues as we stood and held hands with them in the open air. I noticed an older guy sitting on a bench nearby, watching with interest all that was going on. I sat next to him and began to tell him about Jesus. He told me that He was a Christian and had attended a well known Bible school years ago. As he was talking, I sensed that something wasn't right and that He had been abusing children. I didn't want to come right out and say it to him, so I chose my words carefully. I said, "Jesus loves you so much and He wants to set you free from the sin that binds you." He didn't hear me, so I repeated it, but each time it was as though he hadn't heard a word I'd said. I felt that there was a demon covering his ears. "I am like the deaf who cannot hear, like the mute, who cannot speak; I have become like one who does not hear whose mouth can offer no reply" (Psalm 38:14).

I looked him in the eyes and said, "I bind the evil spirits in this man that are stopping him from hearing the truth" and I repeated the fact that Jesus loved him and wanted to set him free. That time he heard me. But he replied, "I know I am in deep sin but I don't want to be set free" and then walked off. I spent all that night praying that the Lord would save his soul.

Deliverance is Not Meant to be a Specialised Activity for 'Experts'

We should get used to casting out demons as much as praying for the sick or giving prophetic words. It should be part of the normal Christian life. Regularly in our shop, 'Spirit', or in 'Café Life', we cast out demons over a coffee with other customers nearby. It isn't supposed to be something that's done behind closed doors. Reading the accounts of Jesus casting out evil spirits in the Gospels, He would regularly cast out demons in public places. In Acts 5, we read how Philip cast out demons during the revival that took place in Samaria and as they came out with loud shrieks, many were saved. It is a demonstration of the power of God and it is such a privilege to see people healed and set free who have been under the power of Satan for so long.

Learning the Signs

Learn to recognise the ways in which demons manifest. This can happen in a church meeting, at work, in the street, in a supermarket, whilst you're praying for them, talking about Jesus or basically anywhere that the person comes into contact with you, a follower of Jesus. From my own experience, I have noticed various things. The person may look confused or hot and start sweating, they may have an intense pain in the head, rub their arm, run away, begin to argue, shout, look like they are going to vomit, fall asleep or any other unusual reaction. As soon as you see something like this, ask them what the problem is or what they're feeling. They will usually be open with you and tell you they have a sudden headache or they need to leave quickly or they have a strange sensation in their legs or may feel faint. I would then ask if it feels good or bad. If it's good I explain it's probably the Holy Spirit, the presence of Jesus they are feeling. If it's bad, I tell them that the presence of Jesus is making any evil spirits uncomfortable.

Treat the person with love, respect and compassion. You do not need to shout or become violent. Your authority is in Jesus, not in the volume of your voice. Discerning spirits is as much about discerning the person you are ministering to as much as the spirit you are dealing with.

I tell them that it's easy to be free from the evil spirits through the power of Jesus. I explain that Jesus is God and He died on the cross and took all their sin, sickness and pain and rose again, having beaten death, Satan and every evil spirit. So through the name and blood of Jesus, we can be set free and come out of Satan's Kingdom of darkness and into God's Kingdom of light. You may need to bind any demons that are making the person deaf, confused or feeling ill whilst you tell them this. But normally the person is able to understand the simple gospel message and when I ask if they would like to make Jesus Lord of their life and be set free from evil, they readily agree.

Breaking Strongholds of the Enemy

Once the person has expressed a personal desire to know Jesus I ask them to renounce anything they have been involved with that is not of God, any previous occult practices, religions and sinful behaviour and ask God's forgiveness, encouraging them to do this out loud. If they need to forgive someone I help them do this too. Unforgiveness is a major block to freedom and healing. Then I help the person tell the evil spirits to leave and then to ask Jesus to come in. It's as simple as that! Watch how their face changes from sadness, torment and anxiety to joy, peace and wonder. This should happen on a regular basis, wherever you are.

Helping People through Deliverance

Normally I prefer to encourage the person to tell the demons to leave and you can guide them through this. I generally command demons to leave whilst the person is telling them to go, although if they have been involved in occult practices or are severely demonised for other reasons, you may need to take charge and cast out some evil spirits before that person is able to do it for themselves.

I have helped people be rid of demons and witnessed them leaving in various ways. For example by coughing, throwing up (often a mucus like substance comes out), sneezing, yawning, nose bleeds, farting, pain in the ear, headache, pain in the arm, up from the stomach and out the mouth with shrieks, and many others. So don't expect to follow a formula. Whilst you are praying with someone, keep asking them how they're feeling and what they're sensing. This can help you know what to do next. Always do this through love and continue to reassure them of God's love.

Simple Faith

One word of wisdom: Simple faith and belief in the power of the cross of Christ is everything. Sometimes, though not often, deliverance, particularly from occult involvement, may take time. However, be on your guard against situations where people seem to get stuck in a place of needing perpetual deliverance. It's as if they see their own faith as powerless and deliverance as something which must be done for them. Sometimes the issue here is not primarily one of demonic influence but of taking personal responsibility to believe in the finished work of the cross and apply the blood of Jesus by faith. Deliverance will allow you to do that, but it will not do that for you. As Derek Prince wisely said, "God will only deliver you from your enemies, not your friends."

A committed member of our church family used to be a psychic medium, reading tarot cards and practising reiki healing until he came into our café one day and met Jesus. Without anyone telling him to, he shredded all his occult literature and his tarot cards. The last tarot card he shredded was the devil holding two people like puppets on strings and he felt he had been like one of those puppets, but not anymore! We then prayed with him as he told his 'spirit guides' to leave in the name of Jesus. He watched these spirit guides turn into demons as they left. There was no noise, no power struggles, just peace as he was set free by the blood of Jesus. I love helping people get free. Why not step out in faith the next time an opportunity presents itself to you? Jesus told us to. It's so much fun.

Chapter Seven

Light in the Darkness

*"Arise, shine for your light has come and
the glory of the Lord rises upon you"*

Isaiah 60: 1

A Satanist contacted me on Face Book. She used a Satanist name so I asked the Holy Spirit what her real name was. The first thought that came to mind was 'Susanna' so I wrote, "Hi Susanna. I don't think I know you; have we met?" She told me that I was known to them and they were watching me. She could not talk with me in person for her own safety. I told her I was praying for her and to let me know if I could help her in any way. She said she had sought me out and got hold of my book, 'A Diary of Miracles'. I asked her how they had heard of me and she said, "We are dedicated, unified, hard working people who wish to serve our lord every moment of every day, everything we do, we do for him. We study our enemy, we take pride in knowing what is within our grounds, what we need to shield, and who we have to 'watch'. I heard... I found it (my book), I started to read it, to learn, to study, and in that, my mind asked itself 'would she even consider talking to someone of my kind?'"

7-28-19 (Mon.)

She told me that she needed help; how she had been a Satanist for years but a close friend, also a Satanist, was tormented from past abuse and screamed through the night with terrible nightmares. She also told me that all his fingers were broken. She was worried about him.

She said she had prayed to her god for help but he hadn't helped, it seemed to make her friend worse, that Satan wanted to keep him like that as a power source. "This is why I have betrayed my family here, and have spoken out, to your kind." After studying my book (and of course reading about all the miracles Jesus is doing), she wondered if my God could, or would help. She would not dare meet me for her own safety, but we conversed via Face Book. I told her that my God, my Jesus would help and I asked Jesus to visit her friend that night and that her friend would put his broken fingers into Jesus' wounded hands and be healed.

The next day she sent me a message saying, "He slept Aliss. This is ... this is shocking to me. He slept with no bad dream. AND, his fingers are, well the swelling is reducing... Your Jesus, would do this, for him? Why? I do not understand what is happening..., I am stunned!"

I explained to her that Jesus loves her and her friend very much, and that He died on a cross for them. She wrote saying a lot of what they do is about revenge. She also said that someone knew of our conversation. I had heard about Satanists being tortured and even killed if they tried to leave the 'brotherhood'. She said that her guardian knew of our conversation. I guessed she meant a demon. She said she may face death because of it. I told her to call on the name of the Lord Jesus, as whoever calls on His name shall be saved.

The last thing she wrote to me was, "Somehow, after many years, I have come to lose the command, and the brotherhood." A few days later I received this message from her Face Book account, "I am a friend of (the Satanist who had been contacting me). I have sad news - she was found dead this morning 3.30 am."

She had lost her life because she had sought out Jesus. "Whoever loses their life for my sake will find it" (Matthew 10:39). I later learned that her name was Sue, so I was probably right in calling her Susanna. She had contacted me as she wanted Jesus to help her and her friend. I believe she has gone to be with Jesus.

I later found out that a friend of mine had a dream in which she was taken into a cave-like place where she observed a secret council praying against Christians. She came out of the dream and asked the Lord to expose the secret council. It was only a few weeks later that the Satanist contacted me to ask for help.

Strategic Warfare

"Councils of the wicked" are being held in secret across our nations, plotting, planning, cursing and forming strategies. It is time for these to be exposed. The Lord is calling His warriors to rise up and uncover and expose the plans of the enemy and for the councils of the Lord to take place to find out His plans and strategy at this time. The Lord wants to give us specific information in order to equip us and show us what to do, where to go, who to link up with and what to say at each moment of our lives.

I love the way in which the prophet Elisha in the Old Covenant was able to warn the King of Israel of his enemy's plans because Elisha could see and hear what was being plotted and he uncovered it by the Holy Spirit. The King of Aram was enraged and thought that one of his officers must be a traitor until he found out that "Elisha, the prophet who is in Israel, tells the King of Israel the very words you speak in your bedroom" (2 Kings 6:12). How much more should we who are under the New Covenant through Jesus, be able to see what Satan is planning for us and our nations? Do not worry. "Take heart! I have overcome the world," declared Jesus (John 16:33b).

Increasingly, those currently living in deep darkness and wickedness will flock to the light of the glory of the gospel of Jesus. Jesus died for all of us and that includes all those involved in Satanism, Witchcraft, New Age practises and Spiritualism. Jesus loves each one of them and gave His life for them. We need to help these people escape from the Kingdom of Darkness and come into the wonderful light of the Kingdom of God, through Jesus Christ.

"For you were once darkness, but now you are light in the Lord. Live as children of light (for the fruit of the light consists in all goodness, righteousness and truth) and find out what pleases the Lord. Have nothing to do with the fruitless deeds of darkness, but rather expose them. For it is shameful even to mention what the disobedient do in secret. But everything exposed by the light becomes visible, for it is light that makes everything visible" (Ephesians 5:8-14).

Be the Light

We do not need to look far to know that darkness is all around us, but the glory of the Lord rises upon His children and the darkness has to flee as the light appears. Just as a light switch is flicked on and the darkness instantly disappears, so it is with us. When the light appears the darkness flees. We are carriers of light. We are the light (see Matthew 5:14). The sons of God are rising up on the earth and being made known in the nations. As we recognise the power and authority we carry through Jesus, the glory will begin to glow out from us and expose the works of the enemy.

The prophet Isaiah exhorts us to, "Arise, shine, for your light has come, and the glory of the Lord rises upon you. See, darkness covers the earth and thick darkness is over the peoples, but the Lord rises upon you and his glory appears over you. Nations will come to your light, and kings to the brightness of your dawn" (Isaiah 60:1-3). The last verse of that chapter states, "The least of you will become a thousand, the smallest a mighty nation. I am the Lord; in its time I will do this swiftly" (Isaiah 60:22).

Under the Old Covenant, the glory of God shined so brightly from Moses' face that a veil had to be placed over it. How much more should we, the people of the New Covenant, be glowing with the glory of God. Increasingly we will see followers of Jesus begin to glow and radiate the glory that they carry. "For God, who said, 'Let light shine out of darkness,' made his light shine in our hearts to give us the light of the knowledge of the glory of God in the face of Christ" (2 Corinthians 4:6).

In order for this to happen, we must learn how to be continuously filled with the Holy Spirit and to affect the spiritual atmosphere around us. In most things, we learn by making mistakes and taking small steps forward. This is the same in the spiritual realm. We must understand that, "… though we live in the world, we do not wage war as the world does. The weapons we fight with are not the weapons of the world. On the contrary, they have divine power to demolish strongholds…" (2 Corinthians 10:3). We must learn how to operate in the spiritual realm. I continually ask the Holy Spirit to show me what is happening in the spiritual realm and I ask Him to teach me every day. I am not a fast learner, and I make many mistakes, but gradually I begin to understand what He shows me by stepping out in faith and having a go. Usually it is not until I have attempted to do something that I understand more fully what is happening, and perhaps what I should have done or said!

The more we do this, the more the glory in our lives will be revealed in the spiritual realm and in the physical realm. I want to share with you some more stories, times in my life where I have begun to learn more about the spiritual realm.

Tormenting Spirits Uncovered

Early one Sunday morning, soon after we had started up our new church in Blacon, Chester, I was preparing for speaking at the meeting that day. I asked the Holy Spirit to give me words of knowledge for people who would be there in the service. I was alone in my bedroom but I heard something moving in the wardrobe next to my bed. It sounded as though someone was moving all my shoes around. Then a similar noise occurred at the foot of my bed. I wasn't scared, but I was rather curious. Later that morning after I had preached, I said, "Is there anyone here who has strange things happening in their house, like a poltergeist?" A woman sitting on the back row whom I did not recognise, raised her hand and said, "Yes, it's me." She came out to the front and told us that there was a poltergeist in her home that had been there for the past three years. She was so scared she'd decided to go to church that day to see if God could do anything. She had also arranged for a psychic medium to call round at her house that afternoon to try and cleanse it.

I explained to her that if she gave her life to Jesus, the demonic activity in her house would stop, so she did. She went home, prayed round her house and telephoned the psychic medium. She cancelled her appointment and told him that his services weren't necessary as she had now found Jesus and said, "What you are doing is wrong, you need Jesus too." Needless to say, she has not experienced any demonic activity in her house since.

I later realised it must have been an angel in my bedroom that gave me a word of knowledge that day.

Manifest Intimidation

Soon after we decided to move to Blacon, the neighbourhood where we planted the church, a demonic principality appeared to me in the night. It stood on the roof of our neighbour's house and tried to intimidate me. I later asked the Holy Spirit what it was and what I needed to do about it. He told me it was the 'Prince of Blacon' who was scared because of what we were doing and that I wasn't to confront it, but to just do what I was called to do – preach the good news of the Kingdom of God, heal the sick, cast out demons, worship etc - and we would see it fall. I realised that demons often manifest when they're scared, something we need to get used to but not be intimidated by or become focused on.

Sweeping the House Clean

My friend and I were prayer walking in our neighbourhood some years ago. The Holy Spirit showed us which house to visit, so we knocked on the door, not really knowing what we were going to see or who we were going to meet. A lady opened the door and instantly I imagined a black cloud hovering over her head. I later realised it was an evil spirit. We told her we were Christians and that Jesus had told us to knock on her door. She said that she was tormented and was just about to commit suicide! She was so glad we had come. She invited us in and told us that there was a dark cloud over her head and another one in the room. We told the evil spirits to leave, shared with her about Jesus and went on our way.

The next day I received a phone call to say that she had been admitted to hospital as she was hearing voices and was very disturbed. I realised that we had not led her to Jesus. Without the light of Jesus on the inside of her, the demons would be likely to come back with some of their friends and she'd be worse off than before (see Matthew 12:43-45).

I felt awful. I told the Lord I was sorry but realised I had learned something that day. Soon afterwards that lady came to our group and gave her life to Jesus. She is still connected with our church family and doing well.

Demonic Reactions

A guy came into our café one day. I'd seen him around a few times. In fact each time I saw him I noticed he was sweating and looked distressed. I realised that he was demonised. I asked him if he'd like me to pray for him. He was fearful but eventually let me put my hand on him. I released the love of God and the power of God through the Holy Spirit. He began to sweat even more and his body shook. He pulled away and said in a strange voice, "You've got the power of God. You've got the power of God!" I said, "Well, yes." I realised it was a demon speaking to me. He ran out of the café, obviously shaken.

The next time I saw him he told me what had happened. He said as I put my hand on his shoulder he felt an intense heat, like fire. He felt his spirit come out of his body, high into the room and then back again. He said never before had he experienced such a feeling of love. He asked me to do it again. A few months later he came rushing into the café, just as a homeless guy who we'd fed was being healed of pneumonia and trench foot, and he declared, "If there was ever a time I need healing, it's now!" He meant that he needed to be free of evil spirits, so we prayed with him, he told them to leave and he asked Jesus to come into his life. We saw an immediate change in him.

Know Your Enemy

Many people, including Christians, live under the influence of demons for lack of knowledge about them and the way the enemy works. A handful of times I have experienced demons trying to influence my life and thankfully recognised what was going on straight away and was able to deal with it. I will share some examples with you.

Once I was sitting in the garden on a lovely summer's day with my feet up, reading a magazine. A dark feeling came over me for no apparent reason. I began to feel sad and then depressed quite quickly. I was starting to take on board the depressing thoughts and felt very low, but instantly I realised these were not my thoughts and that I mustn't take them on board or agree with them. I realised a spirit of depression or despair (see Isaiah 61:3) had tried to settle on me, so I spoke out loud and commanded the spirit to leave in the name of Jesus. Immediately the feelings disappeared and I was back to normal. I was shocked to realise that if I'd taken those thoughts any further and come into agreement with that demon, before long I would be suffering from depression. I think this happens a lot to people without them realising it.

Another time whilst we were away at School of Ministry in North Carolina, I was sitting on the sofa chatting to my husband Rob, when out of the corner of my eye I saw a huge black shadow moving across the room and it went behind the sofa. I ignored it, but after a few minutes I told Rob that I was feeling unwell. All my joints began to ache and I felt very tired. I decided to go and lie on the bed upstairs. As I was lying there feeling ill, a thought came into my head, "Satan take me!" The evil spirit had settled on me and wanted me to speak these words out loud; it was quite forceful. I was incredulous and could not believe the impertinence of the thing! I found it difficult to speak but I said, "How dare you. Leave in the name of Jesus now." Instantly I felt fine. I wasn't sure how a demon thought it could get away with being so brazen about it, but I realised I was learning something about the enemy's ways of working.

Understanding the Spirit World

One day in our café, a woman who had been healed of deafness came back in saying she had suffered a stroke. I offered to pray for her and as I told the symptoms of the stroke to leave in the name of Jesus, a guy who had been a Christian for years walked in through the door. A few minutes later he asked to speak to me. He told me that a number of years ago he had a mini stroke and he was having the same symptoms at that moment. He was not aware that I had been praying with a lady who'd had a stroke. I explained to him what was going on, that the spirit that had caused the stroke in the woman must have left her and was trying to attach itself to him. We told the thing to leave and the symptoms left too. What interested me was that he could easily have succumbed to the symptoms and had a mini stroke. I wonder how many Christians are living under something like depression or sickness when if they recognised it for what it was, they could be free through the power of Jesus. The more we take on board the symptoms, feelings and pain, and come into agreement with it, the more the evil spirit has a hold on our lives.

Overcoming Curses

A few years ago, a friend of mine came to my house for a coffee. I went to put the kettle on and she popped to the cloakroom. As I got up, I felt dizzy, I had a pain in my head, my ears became deaf and I couldn't see properly. I thought I must have stood up too quickly, but as she came back into the room, my friend described the very same symptoms that were also happening to her. We decided it must be a demonic attack, so we prayed together and told it to leave. As she was talking, I could only see half her face. It was very strange. The symptoms left after we prayed, apart from the fact that we both had a bad headache.

After a while my friend left, but the pain in my head grew worse, so I lay down on the sofa and fell asleep. I awoke half an hour later, but the headache was still there. I decided it was an evil spirit that was causing it, so I stood up and commanded it to leave in the name of Jesus. As I did so, there was a loud bang on the upstairs window and a woodpecker fell to the ground, dead, outside the patio windows near where

I was standing. I was astonished. I realised that the evil spirit left me, entered the woodpecker and caused it to die. The bird was on its back with its legs in the air, it looked very dead as though it had broken its neck. Now, I like birds, but I don't like to touch them. I wanted to raise it from the dead but wondered if I was supposed to lay hands on it and I didn't want to. I was debating this for a few minutes before I did anything.

I remained inside, looking through the patio windows and didn't touch it, but I spoke out loud and said, "I command the spirit of death to leave this bird now, in Jesus' name." Instantly the bird's body came back to life, it turned over and stood up, blinking its eyes at me. I could hardly believe it and laughed out loud, however the woodpecker remained there for at least five minutes. I thought it would be ironic if a cat came round the corner and gobbled it up, so I said, "In the name of Jesus, fly." It flew off into a tree. I wondered if someone had sent a curse, maybe a curse of death, and even though as Christians we know the blood of Jesus protects us, I believe we need to use that power proactively and apply it to situations and people by confronting things and speaking out loud.

The Power of Testimony

Funnily enough, a couple of years later, just before I was going out to speak to a group of people about Jesus, I was in the sitting room with my son and I said to him, "What do you think the Holy Spirit wants to do in the meeting?" Suddenly two woodpeckers appeared in the tree outside the window. It reminded me of the woodpecker that had been raised from the dead and I thought I should tell the story at the meeting.

Later, after I'd recounted the story, I asked if there was anyone in the meeting who had similar symptoms to those my friend and I had experienced and thought perhaps there would be two people as I had seen two woodpeckers that day. Two ladies raised their hands so I called them out. They had been suffering with similar problems; dizziness, deafness, disorientation and headaches for a few months. One of them could remember when it began and said that she'd had a weird experience. Once they realised it was demons, they both seemed relieved, so we told the demons to leave and instantly they were both healed.

I mentioned all this to another group I was speaking to more recently, and a young man sitting in the corner began to look agitated. He explained that he had been experiencing similar symptoms every month for years since he was a child. We went over to pray for him and as we told the demon to leave he began to have a nose bleed. This sometimes happens, although not very often. He said he felt so much freer and I believe he was healed that day.

Revealing of the Sons of God

It is time for the plans of the enemy to be uncovered, for the light to shine and the darkness to be exposed. "For the word of God is living and active. Sharper than any double-edged sword, it penetrates even to dividing soul and spirit, joints and marrow; it judges the thoughts and attitudes of the heart. Nothing in all creation is hidden from God's sight. Everything is uncovered and laid bare before the eyes of him to whom we must give account" (Hebrews 4:12).

The Word of God declares, "As many as received him, he gave the right to become children of God" (John 1:12) and "Because you are sons, the Father has sent forth the Spirit of his son into our hearts crying Abba Father. Therefore you are no longer a slave but a son, and if a son, then an heir through God" (Galatians 4:6,7). "The creation waits in eager expectation for the sons of God to be revealed" (Romans 8:19). If you follow Jesus then you are a son of God and have been made a joint heir with Christ. Come on, it is time for the sons of God to be made known in this world. It's time to rise up and shine with the light of the glory of God. Affect the atmosphere everywhere you go. No longer feel oppressed by the spiritual atmosphere of what is going on around you, in your work place, your home, your neighbourhood. Rise and shine for the light has come. Jesus came to earth as the light. He ascended to Heaven and is back with the Father. You are the light of the world now, because of Who resides within you. The Kingdom of Heaven is within you. Let it out! We must be about the Father's business just like Jesus was.

"Overwhelming astonishment and ecstasy seized them all and they recognised and praised and thanked God; and they were filled with and controlled by reverential fear and kept saying, "We have seen wonderful and strange and incredible and unthinkable things today" (Luke 5:26 AMP). May that be said by the people you come into contact with each day.

Jesus said "I have given them the glory that you gave me" (John 17:22). We are carriers of the glory. Let the light of the glory shine out and see what "wonderful, strange, incredible and unthinkable things" happen around you!

Chapter Eight

Healing

*"The sun of righteousness will rise
with healing in its wings"*

When I was a child I watched transfixed as a young boy's deformed leg miraculously changed from being twisted to straight and grew out right before my eyes. A visiting healing evangelist had called the children forward to help pray for this boy whom we knew well. It was clear to me then that Jesus still did miracles. I'd seen it. Over the years following that healing, I read the gospel stories of Jesus performing miracles and never once doubted that they were true. But I couldn't remember praying for anyone after that and having any success.

I was around thirty years of age when I began to think of those days, that as a young teenager I witnessed people being healed and set free from demons. I decided it was what I wanted to do. I read again the gospel stories and began to study Scriptures about healing. I found there were books on revivalists of the past who had remarkable healing ministries. I loved reading stories of how they began their ministries and the many testimonies of those healed. "If they could do that then," I thought, "there is no reason why we can't do that now. Jesus is the same yesterday, today and forever."

For almost twelve years I prayed for people for healing; on the street, in church, sometimes at work or in supermarkets. And during those twelve years I didn't really see any miracles. Occasionally I felt I was close to seeing a breakthrough in healing and I will tell you about some of those times.

French Supermarket

One summer we went away to the South of France with some good friends and our respective children. It took us a couple of days to drive down there but that was all part of the fun. We were staying in a holiday park with a communal pool. The weather was hot and we were having a wonderful time. One day we went to the supermarket. Our friends took me with them in their car and my husband Rob stayed with the kids.

I was pushing my shopping trolley (cart) around the French supermarket and just as I was looking at the cheeses, a woman walked past, pushing a trolley with a young boy in it. Hearing aids dwarfed both his ears. My heart went out to him and I said, "Lord, do you want to heal that boy?" (I'd previously heard teaching that we should ask God if He wants to heal someone first. Now I know that it's God's will to heal all!).

Very clearly, I felt the Lord say, "Yes of course I do." By then, the woman had walked past and disappeared into another aisle. I thought, "OK, well if you arrange for them to be at the checkout the same time as me, I'll pray for him." Half an hour later, after I had paid for my groceries and was heading towards the exit, I saw the woman with the boy and she was walking right next to me! I couldn't get out of it now, so I quickly tried to recollect any French words that I could remember from school that might help me converse with this woman!

I looked at her and began, "Excuse-moi." I used my hands and pointed to the boy and said, "Le garcon, non écoute." All I could remember was "Écoute avec Jean-Paul and Claudette" from my 1980's French lessons, but it seemed to be helping slightly. I pointed to the sky and said, "Jesus" in a French accent, clasped my hands as though praying and then pointed to the boy's ears. After a while the woman seemed to understand what I wanted to do.

I motioned for her to take the boy's hearing aids out. I decided to put my hands on his ears, but discovered I could not remove my hands from the shopping trolley. Power like electricity was flowing down my arms and I found I couldn't control my hands. I somehow eventually moved my hands from the trolley but by now they were vibrating so fast it was almost comical. They were out in front of me and I had to use all my willpower to get my hands onto the little boy's ears.

The mother motioned to me that he was two years old and had been deaf since birth. Finally my hands fixed upon his ears and I commanded the ears to open up in the name of Jesus and for him to be healed. I tentatively decided to test out to see if the boy could hear. I managed to click my fingers next to one ear and the boy turned around quickly to see what the noise was. I was amazed. I had felt the power so strongly coming out of my hands. I was sure that he was healed. However, the mother tapped her watch to indicate that she was late for something, thrust the hearing aids back into his ears and left the supermarket. I was stunned.

I was so sure that he was healed, but it wasn't confirmed. My heart sank. For years I had prayed for God to use me to heal the sick. I had prayed and cried through many long nights. I had fasted and pro-claimed Scriptures and done everything I knew to do. Now, for the first time it looked as though I may have had a breakthrough, and yet the boy was gone and there was no way of seeing him again or knowing for sure. As I sat in the backseat of my friends' car on the way back to the campsite, tears rolled down my cheeks. I was so sad. But in my heart I knew I had been obedient to the Holy Spirit and that was all that mattered. Many other disappointments lay ahead of me, but I decided in my heart that I would not stop praying for the sick. I would keep going no matter what anyone said or whatever the results were. Jesus said, "Heal the sick" as part of the commission, so I would just keep going. As I sat in the car looking out the window, I felt the Lord say that when they arrived home the mother would realise the boy's hearing was fully restored and there would be rejoicing in their household that day. I prayed she would remember that it was Jesus who did the miracle. I know that I will see that boy again one day.

What I have learned from experiences like these is that rarely do things turn out the way I expect. I have met so many people who wonder why they are not seeing healings, but it often transpires that they prayed for someone once who grew worse or who died and so they stopped praying. They didn't see immediate results so they gave up or became offended or discouraged.

Faith Action from the Word of God

You cannot base your beliefs on circumstances nor on what is seen in the physical realm. They must be based on the Word of God. There are many good books written about healing such as T.L. Osborn's 'Healing the Sick' and F.F. Bosworth's 'Christ the Healer' which are both classic Biblical apologetics for healing. I would encourage you to read these books as they give a clear basis for healing, directly from the Word of God.

One of my favourite verses in the Bible is "Praise the Lord, O my soul, and forget not all His benefits, who forgives all your sins and heals all your diseases"

(Psalm 103:2,3). The message is clear. We must not forget that God forgives all our sins and heals all our diseases. The church has taught for many years that He forgives all our sins when we come to Him by faith, but seems to have forgotten the fact that He heals all our diseases too. The original Hebrew word for all is "kol" which means... you guessed it: "all!" It also means each, every, totality, anything, everything and the whole of.

We know that it is God's will that none should perish, but not everyone is saved. It is also His will that all are well, but not everyone is healed. Just because not everyone is saved, it does not mean that we should not teach salvation or try and lead people to Jesus. The same goes for healing. It is part of the gospel of the Kingdom.

For many years the church has taught the gospel of salvation. There has been much preaching and talk of salvation. This is essential. However, it is only part of the Kingdom of God. More than any other subject, Jesus taught on the Kingdom of Heaven.

Healing for All

Many times we see that Jesus healed *all* who were sick: "Great multitudes followed him, and he healed *all* their sick" (Matthew 12:15). "When evening came, many who were demon-possessed were brought to him, and he drove out the spirits with a word and healed *all* the sick. This was to fulfil what was spoken through the prophet Isaiah 'He took up our infirmities and carried our diseases'" (Matthew 8:16, 17).

Jesus Christ is the same yesterday, today and forever" (see Hebrews 13:8).

These Scriptures are all about Jesus healing the sick, but the Bible is clear that the followers of Jesus also did miracles. "When the crowds heard Philip and saw the miraculous signs he did, they all paid close attention to what he said. With shrieks, evil spirits came out of many, and many paralytics and cripples were healed. So there was great joy in that city" (Acts 8:6-8). Peter and John healed a man crippled from birth. Instantly the man's feet and ankles became strong. He jumped to his feet and began to walk. Then he went with them into the temple courts, walking and jumping, and praising God. (see Acts 3:1-8).

Café Life

One day a guy came into our café in Blacon. He was the brother-in-law of our Kitchen Manager. He told us he had osteoporosis which meant his bones broke regularly. He explained that his little finger was strapped up because it had broken and he had just been to the hospital. He was in a lot of pain. We told him about Jesus, the fact that when He died on the cross, He took all of his sin, sickness and pain. The man said he wanted to pray to Jesus, so we sat in the corner and he asked the Lord to forgive him for his sin and to heal him, because he understood that He had taken it all when He was crucified and rose again. Instantly the man was forgiven and Jesus came into his life. He told me all the pain left his finger so I asked him if he could remove the bandage. He warned me that it would be nasty. He said his finger was completely broken and bent backwards to touch his hand. However, as he unwrapped the bandage, he was shocked to discover that not only had the pain gone, but that his finger was unable to bend backwards and seemed to be perfectly normal. That's my Jesus!

God wants to heal you. Healing is part of the gospel. The miracles that Jesus did were not just to prove His divinity, but to fulfil His commission - the will of God. Jesus commissioned the twelve disciples to heal (see Matthew 10:7-8), He commissioned the seventy two (see Luke 10:9). His commission was given to all who believe (Mark 16:17,18). It was given to the church (James 5:14,15). These commissions still stand.

Years ago I had a remarkable dream. It was long before I had any thoughts of preaching. I was a business woman at the time and had never preached. In the dream I was preaching in a church to a large group of people. The dream was very clear and I still remember it now, many years later. I was teaching about healing in the dream and telling people that the word in the original Greek translation of the Bible for healing is 'sozo.' I went on to explain that the words for deliverance and salvation in the New Testament are often from the original 'sozo' too. Then people in my dream began to be healed and delivered of evil spirits and many were saved. When I awoke I thought it was strange as I had never heard the word 'sozo' before. So I decided to do some research and was shocked to discover that what I had been preaching in my dream was true. I love it when the Holy Spirit teaches us things without having to study!

The same word 'sozo' can be translated healed, whole, saved, delivered. For example, Romans 10:9: "If you confess with your mouth Jesus is Lord and believe in your heart that God raised Him from the dead, you will be saved (sozo)." Mark 6:56: "all who touched him were healed (sozo)." He heals you of sickness and saves you from sin.

Here is an amazing verse. When I first heard someone preach from it years ago, I had to look in my Bible before I was convinced that Jesus really did say it. He was talking about miracles at the time. "I tell you the truth, anyone who has faith in me will do what I have been doing. He will do even greater things than these, because I am going to the Father. And I will do whatever you ask in my name, so that the Son may bring glory to the Father. You may ask me for anything in my name and I will do it" (John 14:12-14). It's almost too good to be true. But it is true. Read that verse a few times and drink it in. Meditate on it and learn it.

Ministry School

A year after the incident with the deaf boy in France, we went as a family to MorningStar School of Ministry (now MorningStar University) in South Carolina, USA and spent a wonderful year there. Whilst there, I was still very keen to pray for people but hadn't seen any instant miracles. I was praying constantly for God to use me to heal others. One day, along with some other students, I was asked to go on a ministry trip with Robin McMillan, who was then the Pastor of MorningStar Church in Fort Mill. I was interning Robin as part of the course. The morning we left, I asked the Lord for a word of knowledge. I wanted to know if there would be someone in the meeting the following day that the Lord wanted to speak to, through me. My right ear became deaf for a couple of seconds, then reverted to normal. I couldn't remember having a word of knowledge like that before, but I guessed it may be for someone with a deaf ear.

The next day during the meeting I asked if anyone had a deaf right ear. A woman stood up and told me she had damaged it. I think she said something was missing and she could not hear. I put my hand on it and I commanded the deaf spirit to leave. Instantly she jumped backwards as though I had punched her, but I was hardly touching her ear. I said, "Oh, I think the deafness just left. Be healed in the name of Jesus." I asked her to cover her good ear and I walked behind her, right to the back of the room. Without using the microphone, I quietly asked her if Jesus had healed her. She said "yes" and started to scream and jump. So did I! We were crying and hugging and thanking Jesus. She sent me an email a few weeks later stating she could still hear perfectly well in both ears.

Soon after this, I received a phone call asking if I would like to be involved in healing at the upcoming conference at MorningStar. Excitedly I said that I would. "Finally," I thought, "The beginning of my healing ministry!" But I was disappointed when I was told that I would simply be sitting in a booth booking delegates onto the healing teams for prayer. I wasn't actually part of the healing teams!

I told the Lord I was sorry for being so full of pride and for feeling miserable about this, and a few days later went cheerfully to sit in the booth. I dutifully took bookings from delegates, and then a co-student, also from England, walked by. I asked her if she needed any healing. She showed me a ganglion on her wrist; a hard lump that had been there for six months and required surgery to remove it. Jokingly I asked, "Would you like your healing now?" She said, "Yes please." I put my index finger on it and said, "In the name of Jesus, go ganglion go!" Immediately I felt the lump shrinking under my finger. We looked and it had almost disappeared. We were so amazed, we couldn't stop laughing. Within a day or two it had completely gone. Jesus is so good. He is faithful. In fact, now that former student and her husband are part of the leadership of our church in Blacon.

Perseverance

However, apart from those two incidents I was still not really moving in healing miracles. But I persevered and undeterred, I kept praying for people. So many times we are tempted to give up, but it is important to press on, whether contending for our own healing or for someone else's. I hardly saw any healings for another three years after those two at MorningStar until the week we opened our café in 2009. Suddenly the healings broke out and went off the scale! God has done such incredible miracles since that time that I can hardly keep up with Him. He is such a faithful God.

The best thing is that many other people are now moving in miracles and healings and hundreds have been miraculously healed by Jesus and given their lives to Him. This would never have happened if I had given up. I was discouraged and disappointed many times and people kept telling me to give up, but I refused to let anything stop me. I believed the Word of God to be true and acted on it in faith. For years I would have been bowled over if someone was healed of a slight pain. Now I'm surprised if someone doesn't get up out of a wheelchair when I pray for them!

Build Yourselves Up

Study the Word of God and what it says about healing. Read other books on the subject as I've already suggested. Step out in faith and pray for the sick. I tend not to pray for God to heal someone, but rather I take authority over the sickness or demon and command it to leave in the name of Jesus. Sometimes I speak to it two or three times before it goes, but it usually takes less than a minute. Practice praying whilst going about your usual routine: in the supermarket, at work, at the school gate, in a neighbour's drive etc. You will find that you don't have time to pray a long prayer.

Release the power of Jesus as you pray. Often you will feel power coming out of your hands (that is the anointing) or waves of the Holy Spirit as He ministers to the person. Be aware of any sensations you may feel in your body as they could be words of knowledge. Share them with the person as the Holy Spirit leads.

The Different Ways of Healing

Often you will feel nothing as you step out in faith and pray for someone, based on the Word of God, but they will still be healed. Other times you will operate under an anointing and may feel waves of the Holy Spirit, so much so that you and/or the person you are praying for may find it hard to stand. There are also gifts of healing (see 1 Corinthians 12). Sometimes you may not feel any anointing or presence of Jesus, but as you step out in faith, the anointing kicks in and other people around you will be healed without you even having to pray for them. This has happened on a number of occasions when people have been waiting to be prayed for in a church meeting. They suddenly realise they are completely well and no-one even touched them or prayed for them. During worship people may be healed, just being in the atmosphere of the glory. This should become common place in everyday life, not just in meetings. It happens in our café and shop: people are healed without anyone praying for them or demons come out of their own accord. Sickness, demons and sin cannot bear being in the glory, the manifest presence of God.

Most people we pray for are healed immediately and remain healed. But occasionally the problem can try and come back a few days or weeks later. It is easy to succumb to the pain or symptoms, particularly if you have been used to the illness for a long time. But it is important to stand your ground. Speak to the symptoms or the pain out loud and tell it to leave in the name of Jesus. Treat it as though it is an evil spirit, or something that is illegal and has no right to try and reside in your body. When Jesus went to the cross He took it, He paid the price, so you don't need to have it. Rebuke it. It may take a while but please do not accept the illness back. God does not allow you to be sick in order to glorify Him any more than He would want you to sin. It is a lie of the enemy. You will find if you take a stand and refuse to give in to the symptoms, they will have to leave. However, if you come into agreement with it, you will find that the illness settles back and is difficult to shift the next time.

Making a Place for Healing

Healings broke out when we opened our café in Blacon, Chester in 2009. You can read the stories in my book, 'A Diary of Miracles Part I.' During the first week there were many broken bones healed, but there have been all manner of healings including multiple sclerosis, deafness, blindness, sciatica, spine problems, torn ligaments, diabetes, arthritis, cancer and many other diseases healed. We opened our shop called 'Spirit' one year later and the same thing happened in there from the day we opened.

One day a guy came into our shop to buy a present for his wife's birthday. I asked him why he limped and he told me that he'd had a car accident thirty years before when he had almost died. He had three crushed vertebrae which were pressing on his spinal cord, he had sciatica and had been in constant pain for the past thirty years. He had also lost four inches in height due to the accident and was told he would be in a wheelchair soon. He had bruising on the brain which caused epilepsy, a reconstructed jaw, he lost all his teeth, had a new top palate and often woke up with a bleeding mouth, numb arms and legs. Undeterred, I told him that Jesus could heal him. He seemed a bit unsure but let me pray for him. We were standing in the middle of the shop with other customers browsing the gifts.

I began to pray and felt the power of God strongly. He was unable to speak due to the power he felt going through his body. My husband Rob had to run and catch him as he was falling under the power. I asked him how he felt and he was so shocked that he began to cry. He was hardly able to speak he was so overcome, but was able to tell us that this was the first time in thirty years that he could feel no pain. He sat down and cried. Before we had prayed I watched him get up out of his seat and it took him a while due to all the pain, but after we prayed I asked him to stand up again and he literally jumped up. He told me that each time he went to the movies it would take about twenty minutes to get up out of his seat, but this time he stood up it took him seconds. He told us that he was taller too. He certainly looked like he had grown a few inches. His mouth became numb as we prayed for a reconstruction of his jaw. He felt heat in it. He then told us that his hands had been shaking constantly since the accident but now they were still. He said he felt drunk, he was stunned and was still crying as the realisation that he could be healed dawned on him. He stayed in the shop for a long time that day and only left because he had to go back to work. Before he left he gave his life to Jesus.

He had just walked out of the shop when in hobbled a lady with a walking stick. She had seen the sign outside for 'Free Healings and Miracles' and had come in to investigate. She had a similar problem to the guy who had just left. She had been involved in a road accident the previous year and her spine was out of place and was in constant pain. She could not walk properly or turn sideways. As we prayed for her she felt so much power that she fell and we caught her. She told us the pain had all left, she began to touch her toes and twist sideways. We caught all this on camera. Then she gave her life to Jesus too.

She put away her stick and showed us a large abscess on her calf, about two inches in diameter. I put my finger on it (on her trousers) and as I commanded it to shrink I felt it moving under my finger which was very strange. Then I suggested she could do the miracle since she now had the Holy Spirit living in her; the same Spirit that raised Jesus from the dead. So she put her finger on it and as she commanded it to disappear it shrank right down to a tiny mark. She also had swollen purple ankles and as we prayed the swelling reduced before our eyes and the colour changed to a pale pink. All this is on video.

Equipping and Releasing

I love the fact that Christians are starting to move in healing. When I go and teach at other churches and conferences people expect me to do miracles, but my aim is to release others into doing miracles. I like praying with non-believers and demonstrating the power of God to them and leading them to Jesus, but if a Christian asks me to pray, I usually ask someone else to pray for them. We have staff and volunteers in our businesses that are regularly healing the sick and we are helping others in a number of other nations to demonstrate God's power everywhere they go.

So I would encourage you to go and pray for the sick, just as Jesus commanded us to. The next time you meet someone who is ill or in pain, pluck up some courage, be bold, tell them you are a Christian and ask if you can pray for them. Make sure you ask them to tell you what they are feeling. They may say they feel heat or a tingling sensation. If the problem doesn't leave straight away, pray again, tell it to leave in the name of Jesus and release healing power through the Holy Spirit. You will be surprised by the results. Let me know. I would love to hear how you get on.

Chapter Nine

Miracles, Signs and Wonders

"He rescues and saves; he performs signs and wonders in the heavens and on the earth"

We are in a time where miracles, signs and wonders are increasing, where people are being awed by God, fearing what they see and not being able to understand it. We are coming into a season where there will be demonstrations of power through the occult, but it will be nothing in comparison with what the followers of Jesus, the sons of God will be demonstrating. All the movies and special effects of Hollywood will not be able to gain attention in light of the special effects and miraculous signs that God will perform through the body of Christ on this earth.

We are in the early stages of this. Warriors of Jesus are currently practising spiritual warfare at a low level but they are learning. People like you and me are being trained by the Holy Spirit as we are obedient to Him to undertake tasks that He requires of us.

Those involved in the occult and New Age movement are well aware of the spiritual realm. They travel and have many encounters in the spirit but they use illegal access to gain entry into that realm. Unfortunately, because of this, the majority of Christians today teach against the supernatural. Typically they will quote scriptures such as "The coming of the lawless one will be in accordance with the work of Satan displayed in all kinds of counterfeit miracles, signs and wonders" (2 Thessalonians 2:9). However, this is no reason that the supernatural is not for today but a proof that it is! Satan only counterfeits that which is true. In other words there must be true miracles, signs and wonders otherwise the Bible would not talk about counterfeits.

We are supernatural beings. We must not be fearful of supernatural experiences. Increasingly, Christians are becoming aware of what is available to them through the Holy Spirit, and in turn are able to demonstrate the Truth to those involved in the occult.

The average person in the West would not normally visit a church in order to find out about the supernatural realm. He or she would most likely visit a Spiritualist or Medium or be attracted to the occult. This should not be the case. It is imperative that as Christians we should have an understanding of angels, visions and dreams, travelling by the Holy Spirit, healing, miracles and prophecy. We should be operating in these things. Let us take a look at some Biblical instances.

Biblical Miracles

"You (God) performed miraculous signs and wonders in Egypt and have continued them to this day, both in Israel and among all mankind, and have gained the renown that is still yours" (Jeremiah 32:20).

"He rescues and he saves; he performs signs and wonders in the heavens and on the earth. He has rescued Daniel from the power of the lions" (Daniel 6:27).

The early church asked the Lord, "Stretch out your hand to heal and perform miraculous signs and wonders through the name of your holy servant Jesus" (Acts 4:30).

"The apostles performed many miraculous signs and wonders among the people" (Acts 5:12).

"God did extraordinary miracles through Paul, so that even handkerchiefs and aprons that had touched him were taken to the sick, and their illnesses were cured and the evil spirits left them" (Acts 19:11).

"The whole assembly became silent as they listened to Barnabas and Paul telling about the miraculous signs and wonders God had done among the Gentiles through them" (Acts 15:12).

Like Pharaoh in Egypt with his magicians and sorcerers, there will be a rise in the enemy's demonstration of power. But just as Moses was "like God to Pharaoh," so will the followers of Jesus, as sons of God, demonstrate God's power and authority to the powers of darkness as they perform miracles, signs and wonders on the earth. The Lord has His people being trained in secret, in the hidden places, but He is beginning to reveal them and the power that they carry through the Holy Spirit. This will not just be one or two "men of God" but thousands upon thousands of warriors, 'dread champions', equipped and armed, passionately in love with Jesus, seeing into the spirit realm, obedient to the Lord's instructions. The fear of the Lord will begin to spread. People will have to choose whom they will follow. "I have set before you life and death, blessings and curses. Now choose life" (Deuteronomy 30:19). It's a no-brainer but still people will choose not to follow Jesus Christ!

The Lord was proven to be God on Mount Carmel through Elijah's demonstrations in order to turn the hearts of the people back to God (see 1 Kings 18:37). In our day we will see demonstrations by the followers of Jesus and show-downs between good and evil that will cause the hearts of the people to turn to God.

Spirit Travel

Elisha's servant Gehazi made a serious mistake. He accepted gifts when he ought not to have and lied to Elisha when he denied taking them. However Elisha told him he knew the truth when he said, "Was not my spirit with you when the man got down from his chariot to meet you?" (2 Kings 5:26). Elisha's spirit had travelled and saw what had taken place, even though Elisha was not there in his physical body.

In the New Testament, it seemed normal for the Apostle Paul to be with his churches in spirit even without being there physically, and to be able to pass judgment and see how they were behaving: "Even though I am not physically present, I am with you in spirit. And I have already passed judgment on the one who did this, just as if I were present" (1 Corinthians 5:3) and "For though I am absent from you in body, I am present with you in spirit and delight to see how orderly you are and how firm your faith in Christ is" (Colossians 2:5).

Jesus is the Access Point to the Spirit Realm

If Paul could do this, so can we! Next time you are praying for someone, imagine yourself there with them, ask the Holy Spirit to take you there, imagine what is happening as you pray blessing and encouragement on that person or that community. Then contact whoever you were praying for and see if they describe the same things that you have imagined. You will be surprised!

We have a legal right to the spiritual realm through Jesus who is the door: "I am the door. If anyone enters by Me, he will be saved, and will go in and out and find pasture" (John 10:9 NKJV).

There is an invitation for us to enter in and encounter the supernatural realms. The Apostle John wrote, "After this I looked, and there before me was a door standing open in heaven. And the voice I had first heard speaking to me like a trumpet said, "'Come up here, and I will show you what must take place after this.' At once I was in the spirit…" (Revelation 4:1).

We have looked at some Scriptures that describe how Elijah and Paul travelled by the Spirit. I know of others who have travelled by the Spirit, but their body has been transported as well as their spirit. The following story is an excerpt from my book, "A Diary of Miracles Part I" which I wrote whilst working in our café in Blacon, Chester, UK…

"A few weeks ago we prayed with Mandy (not her real name) who was healed of a pain in her neck and she almost fell over when she felt the Holy Spirit's presence. She came in today and told us what happened after we prayed for her last time. She drove to Pwllheli in Wales (about two hours away from our cafe) on her own, to meet her family at Haven Holiday Park where she'd been before. She must have entered the wrong postcode into her sat nav (GPS) as five hours later she found herself completely lost, in the middle of Wales with sheep, mountains and no sign of civilisation! It was beginning to get dark and she was starting to panic. She said, "God, I need a miracle. Please get me to Haven Holiday Park in Pwllheli and I'll give my life to you and try and be a good person for the rest of my life!" Suddenly the lights in her car went out, her sat nav turned off and so did her phone. She screamed and slammed on her brakes. Her lights, sat nav and phone came back on and she looked out the window. There in front of her was Haven Holiday

Park! Wow! She had been transported in the Spirit. I told her it was like Philip in Acts 8, although he wasn't in a car! The electrics must have all shut off as she was being taken in the Spirit. That is so cool. Then she told us that a lot of her prayers have been answered and she wants to give her life to Jesus. So she did! We sat around the table, holding hands, as she repented of her sin and asked Jesus to be Lord of her life."

The example I have cited here is of being physically transported. This is going to be more commonplace, although always exciting when it happens. As mentioned in the extract, Philip was holding a revival in Samaria where people were getting saved, demons were coming out of them and many paralytics and cripples were healed. "When the crowds heard Philip and saw the miraculous signs he did, they all paid close attention to what he said" (Acts 8:6). It is the same in our day. You can try talking to people about Jesus but I have found that when miracles, signs and wonders demonstrate the power of God, people pay attention. We see in this account of Philip that even a sorcerer who had amazed the general public with his powers was astonished at the great signs and miracles that he saw the apostles doing. He offered money to buy the power, he was so impressed. But Peter rebuked him for this.

During this time, an angel appeared to Philip and told him to go down to the main road. On his way he met a senior Ethiopian official who was reading Isaiah 53. Philip led him to the Lord and baptised him, and then "the Spirit of the Lord suddenly took Philip away" (Acts 8:39) and he appeared in Azotus.

As well as being taken places by the Spirit, at one point Elijah ran faster than a horse and chariot (see 1 Kings 18:46). Elijah was taken to heaven in a fiery chariot and his dead body was never found. Enoch walked with God so closely that he disappeared from the earth too. If that was under the Old Covenant, how much more should we, partakers of the New Covenant, witness greater things than these.

"Therefore if you have been raised up with Christ, keep seeking the things above, where Christ is, seated at the right hand of God. Set your mind on the things above, not on the things that are on earth" (Colossians 3:1-2).

The Heavenly Realms

We are instructed to seek the things above, to desire heavenly encounters, stretching our thoughts to the spiritual realm where Christ is. We are invited into throne room encounters, to experience visions, revelation, supernatural knowledge and angels, asking the Holy Spirit to show us heaven and take us on heavenly journeys. The more we know and see in the heavenly realms, the more effective we will be on this earth and we will walk in the realms of the Spirit.

The Apostle Paul described a heavenly encounter that he had. "I may as well bring up the matter of visions and revelation that God gave me. For instance

I know a man who 14 years ago was seized by Christ and swept in ecstacy to the heights of heaven. I really don't know if this took place in the body or out of it, only God knows. I also know that this man was hijacked into paradise… there he heard the unspeakable spoken" (2 Corinthians 12:2 The Message translation). I want to experience more heavenly encounters. Here, Paul did not even know if he visited heaven in his body or just in his spirit. It didn't seem to matter to him. He obviously felt that he was there in person.

Trances

Maria Woodworth-Etter (1844-1924) was known for her trances. She was an amazing woman of God; a preacher, evangelist and miracle worker. She would travel hundreds of miles and set up a large marquee to conduct her meetings. She planted many churches. As a woman preacher she was controversial, but the fact that both she and many of her audience would fall into trances that lasted for days, made her even more contentious.

It is documented that those attending her meetings would 'trance out' and lay as dead for hours and sometimes for days, their pulses slowing right down. Many of them would be carried and laid out in the woods or wherever there was space for them until they awoke.

Maria would sometimes fall into a trance in the middle of preaching. She would stand with her hand raised and not blink or move a muscle for hours or even days. I can imagine what the 'heresy hunters' thought of that! But trances are Scriptural. Peter fell into a trance whilst on a roof top and had a vision (see Acts 10). Paul fell into a trance while he was praying in the Temple and saw the Lord speaking to him (see Acts 22:17). Trances seemed to be quite acceptable and normal experiences for the early church.

When I have experienced a trance, it has been almost like falling into a dream-like state where it is so real, but it happens whilst awake, not while sleeping. It is normally when the Lord wants to show His children something important that He doesn't want them to miss.

It was not just in Maria Woodworth-Etter's meetings that people fell into trances. The power of God fell across a whole region whilst she was ministering. One time, a group of young ladies were having a party some seventeen miles away from the meetings. They began to make fun of Maria and mimicked the trances. Suddenly they were struck down by God, falling in real trances as though they'd been shot. The party turned into a prayer meeting and cries of mercy were heard coming from that place as they fell on their faces before the Lord and asked for His forgiveness. I guess that's when the real party got started!

I believe that we are going to see this sort of thing break out too, amongst all classes of people; not just healings but bizarre miracles, trances, people falling, fear of the Lord, holiness, people being swept into the Kingdom en mass. With Woodworth-Etter we see a demonstration of the Kingdom breaking out, from heaven to earth, and this was just through one person. Imagine what will happen when all followers of Jesus begin to move in power like this. The majority of past revivals happened in church meetings or tent crusades. Today we are seeing revival break out in everyday life. Non-Christians do not tend to go to church meetings any more, but miracles are breaking out in work places, in shops, businesses, University campuses and at school gates. This is the normal supernatural Christian life. It is on the increase and nothing can stop it. This great army is arising and will not back down, no-one can prevent it happening but ourselves. No weapon formed against us shall prosper. Jesus has given us authority over all the power of the enemy and nothing can harm us.

Spiritual Fairs

We have friends in Ede, Holland; a whole group of young people in their early twenties who go out on 'wheelchair hunts', praying for people in wheelchairs to be healed. We met them through Juriaan who came to Chester after hearing about our café. He and his friends set up a stall at a 'Spiritual Fair' in Holland and he gave us this exciting report: "This weekend we were at a spiritual market sharing Jesus' love through prophecies, healing, dream interpretation and spiritual cleansing.

A woman in an electric wheelchair passed by. I asked what was wrong and she told me she had a stroke fifteen years ago and since then the left half of her body was paralyzed. She looked really bad and depressed so I thought, 'She really needs some Jesus'. I prayed for the effects of the stroke to be completely restored and when I prayed that, her mind was completely clear. She could concentrate and hear me - that was hard for her before. Then I prayed for her left arm to come alive and after the prayer her arm convulsed. I prayed again and her feeling started to come back. After praying several times she could move her arm by herself. Then we prayed for her leg and after a short time she could move her toes and feeling started to come back in her knees. In half an hour she was completely restored and with some help she could walk by herself.

The next day she came back and showed us she could get out of her wheelchair by herself and walk. I have never seen someone so amazed and happy as her. She hardly could believe it and wondered when she would wake up! Jesus is Lord so sickness had to bow. She brought her sister with her who had scoliosis (twist in her spine). Jesus healed her completely after persisting in prayer… Today I had a phone call from her sister who was healed of scoliosis. She said she is doing well and wants to see me again."

The woman's brother was with her as the healing took place and he began to video the miracle as soon as her arm convulsed. Wonderfully, the video footage continued back in her apartment, so viewers can witness the woman get out of her wheelchair and walk around, giggling as she realised she was able to walk again for the first time in fifteen years. You can watch the video on our website (see back of book for details).

Sarah

Sarah works in our café in Blacon, Chester. She prays for people and witnesses healings on a regular basis as well as leading them to Jesus. She lived in a women's hostel for almost a year when she first arrived in Chester, soon after she gave her life to Jesus. She was nervous but began to pray for the women in the hostel and many were healed and most were saved. I remember one young woman whom she had brought to church. She had come off heroin and was asking for a Bible. I placed a Bible in her hands but she threw it back at me! She asked me to do it again and told me the Bible was literally vibrating. I told her the Word of God is powerful, more powerful than a two edged sword!

Another time Sarah brought two ladies into our café. When I saw them I remembered a dream I'd had early that morning. I was casting out demons and knew the names of the demons. One of the women who Sarah had brought had just come out of hospital as she was hearing voices and seeing demons. We cast out the demons, in fact both of them needed deliverance. We just did this at a table in the café, with other people sitting at tables eating their lunch! The demons that came out had the same names as the demons I'd cast out in my dream. That often seems to happen.

Transforming Lives

I loved reading Jackie Pullinger's book, "Chasing the dragon" which tells story after story of heroin and opium addicts coming off drugs without withdrawal symptoms. We have a café and a church in a large neighbourhood that has a lot of crime and people with addictions but we are seeing the power of God working in people's lives.

There was a woman in our neighbourhood who was well known to most people. She was a heroin addict, an alcoholic, a prostitute, a lesbian, schizophrenic, she had been in prison on numerous occasions, she was violent and a danger to herself and others. She had been on drugs since she was eleven. She is now in her late forties. One day she went to score some drugs but her drug dealer was not in. She sat on the wall opposite our café and wondered what she should do. She was in desperate need of a fix but she heard a voice in her head say, "Go to the café. Go to the café." She had never even noticed our café before, but she got up off the wall and went in. Inside she met Ian who had been a heroin addict for twenty seven years before he gave his life to Jesus in our café the previous year. She asked him for drugs, but he told her he was clean and that Jesus was now his habit. He asked her if she'd like to follow Jesus too. She told him, slightly cynically, that she would and Sarah and Ian prayed with her.

She poured out her heart to the Lord in floods of tears as she felt the full weight of her sin and then the joy as she realised she was forgiven. Instantly she was delivered of her addictions, she forgave people who had hurt her, got free of some demons including her mental illness and realised she found men more attractive than women! Our church helped her to do up her apartment, get a front door and she began to buy more feminine clothes. She was baptised in water and in the Holy Spirit. It has been tough for her remaining in the same environment, with dealers offering her free drugs, but we have witnessed such a dramatic change in her life. Others have too, so much so that her support workers come into our café to get saved and to ask if we can help more of their clients. Many people I meet from the neighbourhood who don't know Jesus have heard that this woman has changed since she met Him. Let's expect to hear more stories like this as we release the Kingdom of Heaven in our world.

Buzz off!

As I am writing this chapter, a big fly came into the room, I told it to leave and it did. One of Satan's names is Beelzebub which means, 'Lord of the flies'. Over the past year I have been practising taking authority over flies and telling them to leave in the name of Jesus. I have noticed that I can even command the fly to leave either by the door or the window and it will do as I tell it. It's very useful to be able to do this, but sometimes I think we forget that God gave Adam dominion over the earth and over the animals, "Be fruitful and increase in number; fill the earth and subdue it. Rule over the fish of the sea and the birds of the air and over every living creature that moves on the ground" (Genesis 1:28).

I am looking forward to walking on water and turning water into wine. When I begin to glow, please tell me! I wonder if you can feel it or if you only notice that you're glowing when you see other people's reactions as you begin to talk to them.

Raising the Dead

I am also looking forward to raising the dead. As I already mentioned, I've raised a woodpecker from the dead. You have to practise these things don't you!?

A number of years ago we heard that someone we knew had died in the night. He had become a Christian a year or so before he died. I think he was only around sixty years of age when he died suddenly of a heart attack without any warning. As soon as I heard of his death, the Holy Spirit's presence came upon me so strongly that I could not stand, but I felt the Lord tell me to go and pray for him to be raised from the dead. I contacted his family and told them I would like to go and pray for him. I could not drive as my legs had buckled and I was shaking under the anointing. My husband, Rob, agreed to drive me there. I was absolutely certain that the dead man would get up and come home with us. I was even planning what I was going to say to the TV crew when it arrived.

We parked at the hospital and knocked on the mortuary door. A guy answered with his scrubs on and a mask and told us to go and wait and he would prepare the body for us. The family had called before we arrived and asked them to let us pray for him. We were escorted into a small room where our friend lay. A mortician stood outside the room and left the door ajar, so he could hear what we were saying. It was very strange. However, we began to speak in tongues and invited the presence of the Lord. We took authority over the spirit of death and told it to leave, and asked for his spirit to come back into his body. There was a real sense of God's presence in the room and we knew there were angels all around. He looked at peace. We continued to pray for half an hour, but he didn't get up. I was so shocked. I think I was more surprised that he didn't get up than I would have been if he had. I couldn't believe it and I was so upset. I felt sorry for his wife and family, but we did everything we could. Rob told me later that he felt that our friend had been given a choice to come back into his body. I can imagine the Lord saying to him, "Look there is Rob and Aliss calling you back into your body. Would you like to go?" I must admit, when I go to be with Jesus, I don't think I will want to come back. Heaven is outside of time and therefore I assume we do not miss our loved ones when we are there.

I have been to the mortuary on another occasion too when my friend's son committed suicide. We prayed for him with a policeman standing in the room watching. I found out later that her son had given his life to Jesus as a young boy, so I think he chose to stay in heaven too. Maybe next time I'll pray for someone who doesn't know Jesus and they will want to come back! I haven't heard much teaching on raising the dead, but our best teacher is the Holy Spirit (see 1 John 2:27). Just do what He tells you and read accounts of people being raised from the dead in the Bible.

Elijah stretched himself out on a dead boy three times in order to raise him from the dead (see 1 Kings 17), Jesus held the hand of a dead girl and told her to get up (see Luke 8) and then her spirit returned to her. On another occasion Jesus called out to Lazarus who was in a tomb and had been dead for four days and he was raised from the dead too. There is no formula or particular words that you should say, but be obedient to the Holy Spirit. In the West, we don't spend much time with the dead. When someone dies their body is normally whisked away by 'the professionals', but in other nations the grieving family are able to spend time with their loved one who has passed away. There are more up to date accounts of people coming back to life in these countries. Unfortunately when people are raised from the dead, the media reasons it as perhaps the person was not really dead, or it was a miracle of 'mother nature', when really it was a miracle performed by a follower of Jesus. But it will begin to happen more often now. There are going to be some spectacular miracles, and it could be you doing them!

John 5:25 "I tell you the truth, a time is coming and has now come when the dead will hear the voice of the Son of God and those who hear will live." The Greek word for Son of God here is 'huios theos' which is also found in Romans 8:19. It is translated there as 'sons of God', that is "The creation waits in eager expectation for the sons of God to be revealed." So in John 5:25 Jesus could have been saying, "I tell you the truth, a time is coming and has now come when the dead will hear the voice of the sons of God and those who hear will live."

In addition, the word 'voice' in the same verse is 'phōnē' in the Greek which means 'a sound, tone, a voice' and comes from the root word 'phainō' meaning to bring forth into the light, cause to shine, shed light, become clear, manifest or appear. This is interesting - as the sons of God (followers of Jesus) are revealed, the dead will live. I think it's time. We have waited long enough.

Strange Phenomena

One day Daniel (not his real name) came into our cafe, a local 19-year-old well known by the police and just about everyone else. He bought some food and went and sat outside. I asked the Lord to send him back in so we could prophesy to him, then watched as he came back for a napkin. We began to prophesy to him; telling him God's plan for his life, that God had called him to be a leader. Then two of his friends came over, plus Daniel's dad, an alcoholic. We began to prophesy and told them about Jesus. We prayed for healing for Daniel's head and the pain left. Then his dad said that his liver was causing him a lot of pain. So we placed our hands on his back and asked for a new liver from heaven. He was amazed as the pain disappeared.

Just then, one of the guys said, "What's that!?" We looked behind them and there was a huge misty fog, like a cloud that just descended in front of the café. It was about one hundred feet long, one end began outside the hairdresser's and the other end of it was past the off licence. It was high too and so thick we couldn't see through it. They asked, "Is that something to do with God!?" I told them it could be a glory cloud as mentioned in the Bible, the presence of God. I couldn't believe it and all I could think to say was, "Who wants to get saved and give their life to Jesus?" All four of them said yes, so I explained it meant giving up their lives and the way they have been living and following Jesus and His ways. They all said that they wanted to do that.

We went back inside the café where people were sitting and eating and we all knelt down in the middle of the room and held hands. They prayed out loud, repeating sentences after me. Then they asked God to forgive them, naming some of their sins, and they asked Jesus into their lives. It was wonderful. The funny thing was that as we were holding hands and they repeated everything I said, the presence of the Holy Spirit was so strong that I let out a "Whoooaaa!" They all repeated, "Whoooaaa" too!

Expect a Miracle

One of our most popular signs in 'Spirit' shop is one emblazoned with the words "Expect a Miracle". As with many other aspects of the normal supernatural life this is an essential attitude for the Christian believer who wishes to live a supernatural lifestyle. Look out for divine interventions, seek out the extraordinary, take time to notice the unusual... in short, expect a miracle!

Chapter Ten

Living the Supernatural Life

"The Kingdom of Heaven is forcefully advancing"

A guy called Terry Fingers came into our café, a few months after it had opened. I hadn't seen him before. He showed me his hands. Four years previously he had climbed through a broken window and shards of glass had become embedded in most of his fingers. He hadn't been to hospital and the glass was still there but too deep for him to get it out. His friend said he'd tried with a Stanley knife but he couldn't remove it, it was so deep. It caused pain and was a problem. I grabbed his hands while he was eating his breakfast! I said, "I command every bit of glass to come out of Terry's body in the name of Jesus," then he carried on eating!

The next day, Terry Fingers came back into the café. He was ecstatic. He said he'd been up all night as tiny pieces of glass were coming out of the ends of his fingers! The funniest thing was that he also had a problem with his foot. He said that for about thirty years he'd had pain in his foot and not been able to walk properly. He'd been to the hospital but they couldn't find anything wrong. Every pair of shoes had a hole in one sole because of the problem. When I prayed for him I told all the glass to come out of his body, and what we hadn't realised was that the problem with his foot was caused by glass.

As I captured him on video, he said, "I got glass in me. You did a prayer for me yesterday and my foot, look at that, all the glass is coming out! I couldn't believe it. The glass is coming out my fingers, the glass in my foot has been there since I was ten; I always thought it was something else. I got glass in my foot when I was ten. I jumped on a bottle off 'The Wagon' wall, (a local pub) thirty years ago and yesterday, after a prayer from your good self in here, in this Jesus café, the next thing I knew I was up 'til six o'clock in the morning, squeezing the glass splinters out my fingers and it got to the point where I actually realised I've got glass in my foot! I always thought it was something else. Thank you, God. I'm made up with that one. I can feel Jesus in my hands." Soon after, he gave his life to Jesus.

For years, I prayed for God to send revival. I read Isaiah 64 and begged God to rend the heavens and come down, for people to turn out in droves to our church services and to get saved in the meetings.

One day I came to the realisation that God had already rent the heavens and come down to earth, born in a stable, despised by men, had given Himself up for me. He had died on a cross, He overcame Satan and all the powers of darkness and hell, sin, death, sickness and pain and commissioned His followers to proclaim the good news of the Kingdom of Heaven. He told us to go and heal the sick, raise the dead and to love and forgive others as we have been loved and forgiven by our Father in heaven.

I realised that whilst I was begging God to do something, He was waiting for me to do as He had told me to. For many years we have been asking God to establish His Kingdom on earth and trying to build our churches, when all the time the Lord has been telling us to demonstrate and preach the Kingdom of Heaven and He will build His church. We have got it back to front.

I discovered that we have the same Holy Spirit in us who raised Christ Jesus from the dead and spoke Creation into being. As we are submitted to Jesus' authority, He tells us to go (see Matthew 28) in the power and authority He has given to us (see Luke 10:19) and that demons and sickness, poverty and pain will bow to us. We are sons of God, full of the Holy Spirit, carrying the glorious Presence of Jesus everywhere we go.

So, instead of praying for revival I decided to start revival wherever I went. From that moment, miracles began to break out: instant healings, demons were cast out, drug addicts were set free, many chose to follow Jesus and supernatural miracles began to happen. Now this sort of thing happens every day, everywhere I go. Of course, I want to see more. I haven't raised the dead yet (apart from a woodpecker) but I've tried a few times. But instead of praying and praying and praying for God to show up, I'm asking the Lord to show me where I missed His instruction, to train me to hear His voice more clearly, to practice acting upon what I think He's saying and what I think He's doing in Heaven, and bringing it down to earth. When you do this you will discover the favour of God is on your life. That's when the fun begins.

Genuine and Counterfeit

The Creation has been waiting in eager expectation for the sons of God to be made known in the earth (see Romans 8:19). It is time.

One day I was in a business meeting with a woman who was not a Christian. In fact, she was involved in New Age practises: angel cards, reiki, yoga, Buddhism and other religions. She was open to the supernatural but had missed the legal entry way in, that is, Jesus. I had to tell her that I wasn't interested in the business proposition she had for me, but I would like to tell her about Jesus. She began to ask questions and then let me pray for her. She stood up and as I began to pray she felt the presence of the Holy Spirit strongly. She asked some more questions and then revealed, "I have been searching for years and today I have found what I've been looking for: Jesus." She renounced all the New Age practises and gave her life to Jesus. She is now in one of our groups learning how to follow Jesus. You do not need to go on a special mission to lead people to Jesus, just learn to do it in your everyday life.

Many people who are not followers of Jesus see into the supernatural realm more clearly than Christians do. This is not how it should be. We are supernatural beings, created as a spirit in a physical body and our spirits will live forever. Just as Jesus did, we need only do what we see our Father doing in Heaven. In order to do that, we have to practice opening our eyes in the heavenly places, in the spiritual realms and bring the heavenly reality into the physical reality.

In 1 Corinthians 14:1, the Apostle Paul urges us to "Pursue the way of love yet earnestly desire the spiritual gifts." Like 1 Corinthians 12:1 mentioned in the introduction to this book, there is no word for gifts in the original text in this verse, although you will probably see it in your Bible. The words translated as 'earnestly' and 'desire' are actually both the same word in the Greek and together they mean to 'burn with zeal or with passion'. It is clear from this verse that the Bible instructs us to passionately desire the spiritual (or the supernatural). But be clear on this: Do not attempt to enter the spiritual realms by any way other than through Jesus Christ who is the door. As you follow Him with all your heart, the Holy Spirit will take you to places that you could not even imagine, and He will show you what is about to take place around you.

Trust your Heavenly Father

Be reassured that if you are seeking the spiritual realms through the Holy Spirit and pursuing Jesus, you do not need to worry about becoming involved in the occult. In the words of Jesus: "So I say to you: Ask and it will be given to you; seek and you will find; knock and the door will be opened to you. For everyone who asks receives; he who seeks finds; and to him who knocks, the door will be opened. Which of you fathers, if your son asks for a fish, will give him a snake instead? Or if he asks for an egg, will give him a scorpion? If you then, though you are evil, know how to give good gifts to your children, how much more will your Father in heaven give the Holy Spirit to those who ask him!" (Luke 11:9-13).

So, Jesus is the door to the supernatural realms of heaven. Knock and it will be opened to you. Seek and you will find the Kingdom of Heaven. Ask and it will be given to you. It is within you.

"So we fix our eyes not on what is seen, but on what is unseen. For what is seen is temporary, but what is unseen is eternal" (2 Corinthians 4:18). The supernatural or invisible realm is superior to the natural or visible realm and it dominates the natural realm, positively and negatively. Faith is anchored in the unseen or supernatural realm. Faith is an action; it is aggressive and forceful. Faith forcefully sees what is in the supernatural realm and brings it violently into being, in the natural realm. "From the days of John the Baptist until now, the kingdom of heaven has been forcefully advancing, and forceful men lay hold of it" (Matthew 11:12).

Bearing Fruit that will Last

Walking in the supernatural is living out of the heavenly realms on a daily basis. It is experiencing heavenly places and encounters with Jesus, but it is also more than this. We need to bear good fruit (see John 15). It is essential to spend time with the Lord, to encounter Him and enjoy what He is showing you. However, if you are seeing into the spiritual realms but do not understand what you are seeing, it is important to ask the Holy Spirit to interpret and show you what to do with the revelation. It is an exciting adventure with Him.

Preach the good news of the Kingdom and you will have fun; you will be blessed. You may be persecuted, but you will still be blessed. Forgive quickly, do not hold grudges, do not take offence, don't let disappointment hold you back. Love your enemies. Fall in love with the Spirit of the Lord, the Spirit of wisdom and of understanding, the Spirit of counsel and of power, the Spirit of knowledge and of the fear of the Lord (see Isaiah 11:2). Be obedient to whatever He tells you to do; this will require supernatural faith.

Be passionate about the Kingdom of Heaven. Be as "a man who finds hidden treasure in a field. He is full of joy, sells all he has and buys the field" (Matthew

13:44). The Kingdom of Heaven is our home, it is within us and we are to tell people about it with passion and demonstrate it with power, "For the Kingdom of God is not a matter of talk but of power" (1 Corinthians 4:20).

Remember, "The highest heavens belong to the Lord, but the earth he has given to man" (Psalm 115:16). Use the power and authority you have been given by Jesus as you remain submitted to Him. Being full of the Holy Spirit and obedient to Him is key to growing in spiritual authority and power. Sometimes we do or say things that we think do not matter, but perhaps we have ignored those seemingly insignificant promptings of the Holy Spirit and we wonder why we are not seeing more supernatural power in our lives.

It is interesting to note that in John chapter 14 we read some of the last words spoken by Jesus to His disciples, just the night before He died. In verse 11 He talks of the incredible miracles He has done and in the following verse He declares, "I tell you the truth, anyone who has faith in me will do what I have been doing. He will do even greater things than these, because I am going to the Father."

Only a few verses later He says, "If you love me, you will obey what I command." It is imperative to obey everything He tells us to do in order for us to walk in the supernatural power available to us.

Know you have a Purpose and Destiny

Know that you are here for a reason and God has a purpose for your life. Jesus "is the image of the invisible God, the firstborn over all creation. For by him all things were created: things in heaven and on earth, visible and invisible, whether thrones or powers or rulers or authorities; all things were created by him and for him. He is before all things, and in him all things hold together" (Colossians 1:15-17). Jesus is before all things, He is eternal. Ephesians 1:4 says that "he chose us in him before the creation of the world." At the right time, Jesus came to the earth and was born. He had a destiny, a purpose for coming to the earth. The same applies to you. He knew you before you were born and at just the right time, it was ordained that you be born on this earth. We were born as a spirit in a human body at just the right time; you are in the right season. You were born for such a time as this.

As Jesus was growing up, I wonder when He discovered who He was and what His mission was? As a Jewish boy learning the Scriptures, He would have read and memorised the prophets foretelling of a Messiah. Each time He read a prophecy about the coming Christ, did it seem as though He was reading His own life story? We are like Jesus; children of God born on this earth for a purpose. We must discover who we are and what our assignment on this earth is. Jesus walked by the Spirit, obeyed the Spirit and did only what His Father asked Him to. That is how we walk out the normal supernatural Christian life and accomplish all that God has planned for us.

We are like ambassadors, sent to a foreign country and bringing the place where we originate from, the Kingdom of heaven, to earth: affecting the atmosphere with the glory and making earth look like heaven.

Build yourself up in the Holy Spirit. Speak in tongues as you walk or drive down the street. Walking is good so you can prophesy and declare over each home or business. I imagine myself as being huge in the spirit and when I walk past people I wonder if they can see the angels towering above me. I breathe out the Holy Spirit and release God's love over people as I walk near them. You can have a powerful impact on the environment around you.

Do Not Give Up

Do not give up, do not become discouraged, keep turning up, keep pressing on. Keep your motives and actions pure ("Blessed are the pure in heart for they will see God" Matthew 5:8).

I encourage you to keep a journal and write down anything significant that happens in your daily life. I keep a separate book for prophetic words that are given to me and my family and I read them often. I pray over the words and also ask the Lord for strategy, such as, "What do I need to do in order for these prophetic words to be fulfilled?"

Each morning as you awake, talk to the Holy Spirit and ask Him what you are to do that day and whom you will see. He will speak to you; it may be a thought or a vision or a dream you had during the night, or it may be through Scripture. Ask Him more questions. If you think He is showing you that someone will give their life to Him, ask Him who it is and where it will be. Write down whatever you get for that day and put it in your pocket or your bag so you can show the relevant people as and when you meet them.

Ask the Holy Spirit for strategy. If you have been praying for revival to come to your workplace or your neighbourhood, ask the Holy Spirit to give you a vision for it, and also for timescales. How are you going to get from where you are now to being in the midst of revival? I asked the Holy Spirit this question about my neighbourhood and He told me to prophesy to people on the streets and to worship and pray. He said to start a church so we did, then to open a café and demonstrate His power. As soon as it opened revival broke out. Now the church has the task of mentoring the new converts, many of whom are ex-addicts. Plan for that.

I was in the supermarket one day, doing my weekly grocery shopping. A woman was walking towards me with her trolley piled high with groceries, children hanging from her skirt and a large surgical boot on her foot. She was obviously in pain and found it difficult to walk. When you know that you have power to heal the sick, it's hard to walk past someone who is in pain without stopping and offering to pray. I plucked up the courage to talk to her and she told me she had broken her foot. I asked if I could pray and told her that Jesus could heal it, but sadly she didn't want me to and hobbled off as fast as she could with groceries cascading and kids in tow!

I felt embarrassed. I looked around and hoped that no-one had witnessed my rejection. I began to feel sorry for myself, and could not understand why she didn't want prayer. Just then, an older man came up to me and declared, "I love your hair!" How sweet, I thought and began to cheer up, thinking how nice of God to send someone to encourage me.

I turned to thank him and noticed he was wearing hearing aids in both ears. I asked him if he would like prayer, but he was so deaf that even with hearing aids he couldn't hear what I was asking him! I decided to go for it anyway, so I plonked my hands on his ears and commanded them to open in the name of Jesus. Startled, he began to say, "What are you doing?" but before I could say anything he pulled his hearing aids out and realised he could hear again! Jesus had opened both his ears. He was astonished! Then I saw that he was using a walking stick so I asked him what it was for. He mentioned something about muscle wastage and he had a pronounced limp.

I asked him to put his hand on his thigh, where the muscle had wasted away and I put my hand on top of his. So there we were, standing in the middle of the supermarket aisle, with my hand on a stranger's thigh, when who should come round the corner but his wife!? In a shrill voice she demanded, "What's going on here then!?" I stammered, "I'm a Christian Minister and I'm praying for your husband's leg," trying to sound as much like a Christian Minister as I could. I certainly didn't look like one! Thankfully she replied that it wasn't a problem; she thought he'd collapsed and I'd caught him! Then she realised he could hear everything she was saying.

I grabbed his stick and told him to walk in the name of Jesus. Off he went, walking up and down the aisle, almost jogging with no limp. The couple hugged and cried and I joined in too. They told me they knew Jesus but I don't think they knew that He still loves to do miracles today.

And Finally...

"I keep asking that the God of our Lord Jesus Christ, the glorious Father, may give you the Spirit of wisdom and revelation, so that you may know him better. I pray also that the eyes of your heart may be enlightened in order that you may know the hope to which he has called you, the riches of his glorious inheritance in the saints and his incomparably great power for us who believe. That power is like the working of his mighty strength, which he exerted in Christ when he raised him from the dead and seated him at his right hand in the heavenly realms, far above all rule and authority, power and dominion, and every title that can be given, not only in the present age but also in the one to come. And God placed all things under his feet and appointed him to be head over everything for the church, which is his body, the fullness of him who fills everything in every way" (Ephesians 1:17-23).

Jesus told us, "As you go, preach this message: 'The kingdom of heaven is near.' Heal the sick, raise the dead, cleanse those who have leprosy, drive out demons. Freely you have received, freely give" (Matthew 10:7). Whatever our calling, our destiny, our career path, our role in life, we are told to do these things as we go. This is the normal supernatural Christian life.

"Do you know someone who would benefit from my teaching and experiences?

Would you like your friends and family to encounter the love and power of Jesus?

Could me and my team train and mentor you as you operate from the spirit realm and move in power?

Would you like to host or run a small group with our help?

Check out our website for more details and find out how our starter kit could transform your world!"

www.SpiritLifestyle.com
www.facebook.com/SpiritLifestyle

Little Mollington Hall

Spiritual Retreat Centre & Guest House

www.MollingtonHall.org

Little Mollington Hall is a beautiful country house dating back to the early 17th century and situated in one acre of gardens close to the historic city of Chester, UK.

Rooms are beautifully furnished in the style of a boutique hotel, all with en suite bathrooms. Guests are welcome to make use of the elegant surroundings and spiritual ministry on offer. Enjoy a relaxing break in this picturesque city, perhaps attend one of our spiritual retreats or workshops.

You may also like these books and audio sets from Aliss Cresswell

www.SpiritLifestyle.com